199 Tests

Englisch 5. – 8. Klasse

Vokabeln und Grammatik

W0379129

199 TESTS

Englisch
5. – 8. Klasse

Vokabeln & Grammatik

Cornelsen
SCRIPTOR

Autorinnen und Autoren dieses Bandes:
Ingrid Preedy, David Clarke, Phyllis Driver, Brigitte Seidl, Brian McCredie

www.cornelsen.de

Bibliografische Information: Die Deutsche Bibliothek verzeichnet diese Publikation in der Deutschen Nationalbibliografie; detaillierte bibliografische Daten sind im Internet über http://dnb.ddb.de abrufbar.

Dieser Band folgt den Regeln der deutschen Rechtschreibung, die seit August 2006 gelten.

7.	6.	5.	4.	3.	Die letzten Ziffern bezeichnen
11	10	09	08	07	Zahl und Jahr der Auflage.

© 2006 Cornelsen Verlag Scriptor GmbH & Co. KG, Berlin
Das Werk und seine Teile sind urheberrechtlich geschützt. Jede Nutzung in anderen als den gesetzlich zugelassenen Fällen bedarf deshalb der vorherigen schriftlichen Einwilligung des Verlags.
Hinweis zu § 52a UrhG: Weder das Werk noch seine Teile dürfen ohne eine solche Einwilligung eingescannt und in ein Netzwerk gestellt werden. Dies gilt auch für Intranets von Schulen und sonstigen Bildungseinrichtungen.
Redaktion: Marion Clausen, Göttingen
Herstellung: Uwe Pahnke, Berlin
Umschlaggestaltung: bunt unbunt, Berlin
Gesamtgestaltung: Dagmar & Torsten Lemme, Berlin
Druck und Bindearbeiten: Clausen & Bosse, Leck
Printed in Germany
ISBN 978-3-589-22145-5

Gedruckt auf säurefreiem Papier,
umweltschonend hergestellt aus chlorfrei gebleichten Faserstoffen.

Inhalt Klasse 5/6

Grammatikübungen

Inhalt Klasse 7/8

Grammatikübungen

Hallo, liebe Schülerin, lieber Schüler!

In diesem Buch sind eine Menge Vokabel- und Grammatikübungen aus dem Unterrichtsstoff der Klassen 5 bis 8 zusammengestellt. Alle Aufgaben wurden von erfahrenen Englischlehrerinnen und -lehrern erarbeitet und erprobt.
Zur schnellen Orientierung sind auf jeder Seite Klassenstufe (5/6 bzw. 7/8) und Aufgabenart (V = Vokabelübung; G = Grammatikaufgabe) unten in der Ecke angegeben.

Eine Auflistung aller Übungen findest du im Inhaltsverzeichnis.
Dort kannst du die Bereiche aussuchen, die du gerade üben willst.

Jede Seite liefert eine Übungseinheit, die in einem Rutsch bearbeitet werden sollte. Oft kannst du direkt auf die Seiten schreiben; manchmal brauchst du auch ein Extrablatt Papier. Die Lösungen findest du auf dem Kopf in der Farbfläche unten auf jeder Seite. Vergleiche deine Ergebnisse genau. Wenn du Fehler gemacht hast, korrigiere deine Eintragungen. Wenn du merkst, dass du etwas noch nicht verstanden hast, schaue in deinem Schulbuch nach oder frage deine Eltern, Mitschüler oder deinen Englischlehrer.

Viel Erfolg wünscht dir die 199-TESTS-Redaktion von Cornelsen Scriptor

Das Datum von heute 11.03.08

1 Meine Familie (Verwandte)

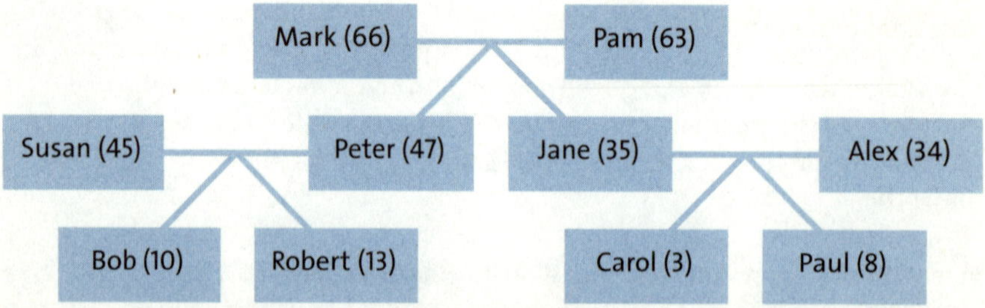

1 Hier sind alle Wörter zusammengeschrieben. Schreibe sie als Einzelwörter und sortiert nach weiblich und männlich auf.

fathersoncousingrandsonbrotherwifesistergranddaughtermotherhusbanduncle grandfatherdaughtergrandmotherauntcousin

weiblich	männlich
mother	father grandfather
dauther	son
cousin	cousin
granddaughter	grandson
sister	brother
aunt	uncle

2 Trage die richtigen Wörter in die Sätze ein.

Jane is Mark's daughter.

Peter is Robert's father.

Carol is Mark's granddaughter.

Alex is Robert's uncle.

V 5/6

1 **weiblich** cousin, wife, sister, granddaughter, mother, daughter, grandmother, aunt
männlich father, son, cousin, grandson, brother, husband, uncle, grandfather

2 Jane is Mark's daughter. Peter is Robert's father. Carol is Mark's granddaughter. Alex is Robert's uncle.

Das Datum von heute 11.05.08

2 Meine Schultasche (Schulsachen)

Löse das Kreuzworträtsel.

Across →

1 Füller
5 Lineal
6 Tasche
7 Kugelschreiber
8 Filzstift
10 Federmappe
12 CD
13 Bleistift
14 Papier

Down ↓

2 Übungsheft
3 Radiergummi
4 Anspitzer
7 Buch
9 Sandwich
11 Apfel

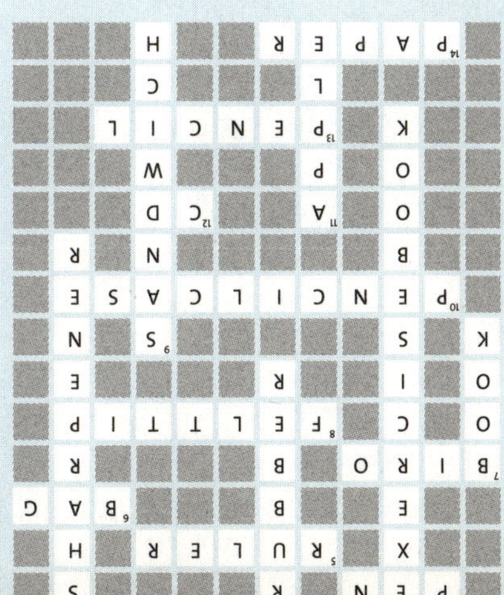

Das Datum von heute 19.02.08

3 Im Klassenzimmer (Schule)

1 Welche Sätze benötigen die Schüler im Klassenzimmer und welche Sätze braucht die Lehrerin? Manche Sätze können von beiden benutzt werden. Kreuze die richtigen Kästchen an.

	Schüler	Lehrer	beide
1 Listen to the cassette.	○	⊗	○
2 Always write nationalities with a capital letter.	○	○	○
3 Could you repeat that word?	○	○	⊗
4 How do you pronounce this word?	○	○	⊗
5 I can't hear the cassette.	⊗	○	○
6 I don't understand.	⊗	○	○
7 Look at / Read the story on page 21.	○	⊗	○
8 Work with a partner.	○	⊗	○

2 Hier sind einige typische Sätze, die du im Englischunterricht hören kannst. Verbinde die passenden Satzteile miteinander.

Please correct ✔ ⟷ your mistakes. ✔

Translate
It's your
Could you please give us
Sorry, I don't
Do these exercises
Could we play
What does this word
Practice
Fill in

for homework.
an example.
a game?
these phrases into English.
the missing words.
the dialogues at home.
remember.
mean?
turn.

1
1 Listen to the cassette. *Lehrer*
2 Always write nationalities with a capital letter. *Lehrer*
3 Could you repeat that word? *beide*
4 How do you pronounce this word? *beide*
5 I can't hear the cassette. *Schüler*
6 I don't understand. *Schüler*
7 Look at / Read the story on page 21. *Lehrer*
8 Work with a partner. *Lehrer*

2 Please correct your mistakes.
Translate these phrases into English.
Could you please give us an example?
Fill in the missing words.
It's your turn.
What does this word mean?
Do these exercises for homework.
Sorry, I don't remember.
Practise the dialogues at home.
Could we play a game?

V 5/6

Das Datum von heute 19.02.08

4 Regeln im Klassenzimmer (Schule)

Der Computer hat hier etwas falsch gemacht. Schreibe den Text richtig auf.

RULES IN THE CLASSROOM:

1 WESAYGOODMORNINGTOTHETEACHERATTHE BEGINNINGOFTHELESSON.
2 WELISTENTOTHEOTHERPUPILS.
3 BEFOREWESAYSOMETHINGWEPUTUPOURHANDS.
4 WEDON'TRUNINTHECLASSROOM.
5 WEDON'TDRINKOREATINTHEENGLISHLESSON.
6 WEDOOURHOMEWORKATHOME.
7 WEAREQUIETINTHECLASSROOM.
8 WEHAVEOURENGLISHBOOKANDPENCILCASEONTHETABLE.

1 We say good morning to the teacher at the beginning of the lesson
2 We liston to the other Pupils.
3 Before we say something we put up our hands.
4 We don't run in the classroom.
5 We don't drink or eat in the english lesson.
6 We do our homework at home.
7 We are quiet in the classroom.
8 We have our englishbook and pencilcase on the table.

1 We say good morning to the teacher at the beginning of the lesson.
2 We listen to the other pupils.
3 Before we say something we put up our hands.
4 We don't run in the classroom.
5 We don't drink or eat in the English lesson.
6 We do our homework at home.
7 We are quiet in the classroom.
8 We have our English book and pencil case on the table.

V 5/6

Das Datum von heute ____________

5 Wie ist es in der Schule? (Schule)

1. What grade are you in now, Bill?
2. When did you finish school, Mr Jones?
3. What was your favourite subject in school?
4. What is your favourite subject in school this year, Bill?
5. Which subject don't you like very much, Bill, and why?
6. Which subject didn't you like very much when you were in school, Mr Jones, and why?
7. When are you most tired in school?
8. Can you remember when you were most tired in school, Mr Jones?

a Latin. It's so boring. People say it's important, but why learn a dead language?

b It was English. I loved it. We had an excellent teacher, and even so many years ago we knew it was important.

c The seventh.

d Maths. I hated it. Maybe it wasn't so difficult then in the 60's, but I just wasn't good at it.

e In 1968.

f I like maths best. Our teacher is great and I love numbers.

g In my first class. Mom says I go to bed too late, but I think I'm just not a morning person.

h Yes, after the last class. I was hungry then, too, and I always had to help my father on our farm in the afternoon.

1 c 2 __ 3 __ 4 __ 5 __ 6 __ 7 __ 8 __

V 5/6

1c 5a 2e 6d 3b 7g 4f 8h

Das Datum von heute ____________

6 Wie viele Schüler? (Zahlen und Zeit)

1 Viele Schüler gehen aus der Schule heraus und wieder hinein. Schreibe die einzelnen Ergebnisse als Wörter auf. Wie viele Schüler sind am Ende noch im Gebäude?

Five + fifteen = ____________ + eleven = ____________ – seven = ____________ + twelve = ____________ – twenty = ____________ + seventy-two = ____________ .

2 Schreibe die Zahlwörter auf.

An hour has got ____________ minutes.

One minute has got ____________ seconds.

An hour has got ________ thousand ____________ seconds.

A day has got ____________ hours.

A year has got ____________ days.

3 Wie spät ist es?

10.00 Uhr It's ten o'clock in the morning.

15.00 Uhr ____________

23.00 Uhr ____________

19.00 Uhr ____________

6.00 Uhr ____________

17.00 Uhr ____________

1 twenty, thirty-one, twenty-four, thirty-six, sixteen, eighty-eight
2 sixty, sixty, three thousand six hundred, twenty-four, three hundred and sixty-five
3 It's three o'clock in the afternoon. It's eleven o'clock in the evening. It's seven o'clock in the evening. It's six o'clock in the morning. It's five o'clock in the afternoon.

Das Datum von heute ________

7 Stundenplan (Wochentage)

Time	Monday				Tuesday				Wednesday				Thursday				Friday			
1 8.00	S	A	T	U	R	D	A	Y				S								
2	U			S	U	N	D	A	Y		U									
3	N							S		S	U	N	D	A	Y		S			
4	D							U				D					A			
5	A		S			S	U	N	D	A	Y	A					T			
6	Y		U					D				Y					U			
7	S	U	N	D	A	Y		A					S	A	T	U	R	D	A	Y
8			D					Y									D			
9			A					S	U	N	D	A	Y				A			
10			Y	S	A	T	U	R	D	A	Y	S	U	N	D	A	Y			

a Wie oft kannst du das Wort *Sunday* auf dem Stundenplan finden? ______

b Wie oft kannst du das Wort *Saturday* auf dem Stundenplan finden? ______

c Trage in den Stundenplan ein, wann die Unterrichtsstunden beginnen.
The first lesson begins at eight o'clock.
The third lesson begins at ten past ten.
The fifth lesson begins at twenty to twelve.
The seventh lesson begins at half past one.
The second lesson begins at five minutes to nine.
The sixth lesson begins at half past twelve.
The tenth lesson begins at quarter to four.
The eighth lesson begins at quarter past two.
The fourth lesson begins at five minutes to eleven.
The ninth lesson begins at three o'clock.

a) 10-mal
b) 4-mal
c) 2) 8.55 3) 10.10 4) 10.55 5) 11.40 6) 12.30 7) 13.30 8) 14.15 9) 15.00 10) 15.45

8 Welcher Tag ist das? (Wochentage)

1 It's the first day of the week.
___ ___ ___ ___ ___ ___
1 2 3 4 5 6

2 It's the day after the weekend.
___ ___ ___ ___ ___ ___
1 2 3 4 5 6

3 Most shops are closed on this day.
___ ___ ___ ___ ___ ___
1 2 3 4 5 6

4 It's the first day of the weekend.
___ ___ ___ ___ ___ ___ ___ ___
1 2 3 4 5 6 7 8

5 It comes after Monday.
___ ___ ___ ___ ___ ___ ___
1 2 3 4 5 6 7

6 The first letter is a W.
___ ___ ___ ___ ___ ___ ___ ___ ___
1 2 3 4 5 6 7 8 9

7 It's the day before the weekend.
___ ___ ___ ___ ___ ___
1 2 3 4 5 6

8 It starts with TH.
___ ___ ___ ___ ___ ___ ___ ___
1 2 3 4 5 6 7 8

9 It's before Friday.
___ ___ ___ ___ ___ ___ ___ ___
1 2 3 4 5 6 7 8

10 It's before Tuesday.
___ ___ ___ ___ ___ ___
1 2 3 4 5 6

11 It's the middle of the week.
___ ___ ___ ___ ___ ___ ___ ___ ___
1 2 3 4 5 6 7 8 9

The children like to watch a

___ ___ ___ ___ ___ ___ ___   ___ ___ ___ ___
1 – 1 **2** – 2 **3** – 3 **4** – 1 **5** – 1 **6** – 2 **7** – 2   **8** – 5 **9** – 2 **10** – 2 **11** – 1

(example: **6** – 2 means: word number **6**, letter number 2)

1 Monday 2 Monday 3 Sunday 4 Saturday 5 Tuesday 6 Wednesday
7 Friday 8 Thursday 9 Thursday 10 Monday 11 Wednesday
Lösungswort: Monster show

Das Datum von heute ____________

9 Der Jahreslauf (Monatsnamen)

December | April | August | June | November | February | July | January | May | September | March | October

1 Jemand hat die Vokale aus den Monaten geklaut.
Schreibe die Monatsnamen richtig auf.

Jnry ______________________ Fbrry ______________________

Mrch ______________________ prl ______________________

My ______________________ Jn ______________________

Jly ______________________ gst ______________________

Sptmbr ______________________ ctbr ______________________

Nvmbr ______________________ Dcmbr ______________________

2 Kannst du diese Monate benennen?

1 The last letter of this month is H:

2 This is the second month:

3 This month has an I in the name:

4 This month is 9 months after *December:*

5 This month is two months before *August:*

6 This is the last month of the year:

7 This is the fifth month:

8 This is the first month:

Die eingerahmten Buchstaben ergeben von oben nach unten dein Lösungswort:

____

1 January, February, March, April, May, June, July, August, September, October, November, December

2 March, February, April, September, June, December, May, January
Lösungswort: calendar

Das Datum von heute ____________

10 Suchrätsel (Geburtstag)

In diesem Suchrätsel sind 20 englische Wörter versteckt. Rahme sie ein.

Die deutschen Wörter sind:
1 KASSETTENREKORDER – **2** GEBURTSTAGSKARTE – **3** EINLADUNG – **4** COMPUTER – **5** CD-PLAYER – **6** KASSETTE – **7** FREUNDE – **8** GESCHENK – **9** KERZE – **10** GITARRE – **11** MUSIK – **12** VIDEO – **13** TASCHENLAMPE – **14** PARTY – **15** COMIC – **16** KUCHEN – **17** SPIEL – **18** FAHRRAD – **19** SPIELZEUG – **20** FERNSEHER

I	N	V	I	T	A	T	I	O	N	Q	C	F	S	N	E
Z	M	A	L	H	C	O	M	P	U	T	E	R	T	X	V
V	I	D	E	O	E	C	A	D	J	E	Z	W	P	S	D
G	A	V	U	C	A	N	D	L	E	U	C	O	M	I	C
I	T	O	R	C	H	M	U	S	I	C	L	O	U	O	F
F	J	T	V	O	G	U	I	T	A	R	I	N	L	O	B
O	F	Z	Y	T	O	Y	P	R	E	S	E	N	T	Z	V
K	U	Z	G	B	I	K	E	E	S	G	A	M	E	A	I
C	A	S	S	E	T	T	E	R	E	C	O	R	D	E	R
S	C	C	H	K	O	I	H	C	D	P	L	A	Y	E	R
V	I	C	A	S	S	E	T	T	E	P	A	R	T	Y	J
K	V	K	S	R	C	A	K	E	K	Y	Q	N	F	P	T
F	R	I	E	N	D	S	L	X	H	R	X	H	J	A	H
Z	B	I	R	T	H	D	A	Y	C	A	R	D	T	P	P

I	N	V	I	T	A	T	I	O	N						
					C	O	M	P	U	T	E	R			
V	I	D	E	O											
			C	A	N	D	L	E			C	O	M	I	C
	T	O	R	C	H	M	U	S	I	C					
		T	V		G	U	I	T	A	R					
				T	O	Y	P	R	E	S	E	N	T		
				B	I	K	E			G	A	M	E		
C	A	S	S	E	T	T	E	R	E	C	O	R	D	E	R
								C	D	P	L	A	Y	E	R
		C	A	S	S	E	T	T	E	P	A	R	T	Y	
					C	A	K	E							
F	R	I	E	N	D	S									
	B	I	R	T	H	D	A	Y	C	A	R	D			

Das Datum von heute ____________

11 Ein Geschenk für Dave (Einkaufen)

Übersetze den Dialog. Hier findest du einige Hilfen:

Mark wants to buy a T-shirt for his friend Dave.
For you? – That's a good price. I'll take it. – Good morning, can I help you? – Here's a nice blue T-shirt. – How much is the T-shirt? – I think *M* is okay. –
It's £9.99. – No, it's a present for my friend. – Thank you. Have a nice day. –
I'm looking for a T-shirt. – What size does he need?

Andy: Guten Morgen, kann ich dir helfen?

(the assistant) ______________________________

Mark: Ich suche ein T-Shirt.

(the customer) ______________________________

Andy: Für dich? ______________________________

Mark: Nein, es ist ein Geschenk für meinen Freund.

____

Andy: Welche Größe braucht er?

____

Mark: Ich denke, *M* ist okay.

____

Andy: Hier ist ein schönes blaues T-Shirt.

____

Mark: Wie viel kostet das T-Shirt?

____

Andy: Es kostet £ 9.99. ______________________________

Mark: Das ist ein guter Preis. Ich werde es nehmen.

____

Andy: Danke. Einen schönen Tag noch.

____

V
5/6

Good morning, can I help you? – I'm looking for a T-shirt. – For you? – No, it's a present for my friend. – What size does he need? – I think *M* is okay. – Here's a nice blue T-shirt. – How much is the T-shirt? – It's £ 9.99. – That's a good price. I'll take it. – Thank you. Have a nice day.

Das Datum von heute ____________

12 Wendy feiert Geburtstag
(Festvorbereitung)

Es gibt viel zu tun. Aber wann was? Hilf Wendy beim Ordnen.

To do:

- write invitations
- decorate the room
- take photos
- play games
- wash the dishes
- dance
- buy coke and lemonade
- make a pizza and some sandwiches
- listen to music
- take the film to the camera shop
- ask mum and dad for the CD player
- take the empty bottles back to the shop

Before the party

____

____

____

____

____

At the party

____

____

____

____

____

After the party

____

____

____

____

____

Before the party:
write invitations, buy coke and lemonade, decorate the room, make a pizza and some sandwiches, ask mum and dad for the CD player
At the party:
listen to music, dance, take photos, play games
After the party:
wash the dishes, take the film to the camera shop, take the empty bottles back to the shop

Das Datum von heute ______________

13 Partyspiel (Wörter sortieren)

1 Wendy hat Geburtstag. Beim ersten Spiel auf ihrer Party sollen die Gäste Wörter sortieren. Hilf ihnen dabei. Schreibe auf jede Zeile zwei Wörter.

road – dictionary – presents – station – hotel – games – classroom – pupils – candles – bus stop – post office – dance – street – decoration – lesson – park – invitation – teacher – shopping centre – computer corner – board – cake – bookshelf – department store – timetable – desk – music – museum

school

____
____
____
____
____
____
____

town

____
____
____
____
____
____
____

my party

____
____
____
____
____

2 What do Wendy's friends say when they come to her party?

H______________ b______________________, Wendy!

V 5/6

1 **school:** dictionary, classroom, pupils, lesson, teacher, computer corner, board, bookshelf, timetable, desk
town: road, station, hotel, bus stop, post office, street, shopping centre, park, department store, museum
my party: presents, games, candles, cake, dance, decoration, invitation, music

2 Happy birthday, Wendy!

Das Datum von heute __________

14 Der Mann vom Mars (Gebäude)

1 Finde alle Namen von Gebäuden in dem Kasten und schreibe sie richtig auf.

AM~~MUSEUM~~BHGTCHURCHKLPSCHOOLASBOOKSHOPFHOTELNMEKTHJPOSTMJOF-FICETHJURNGRESTAURANTMJDEPARTMENTHGSTORESKFHBANKMMHSUPERMAR-KETKLFSWIMMINGKOOPOOLLLSTATIONWERTOYFHSHOPDHFDISCOJEGTSHOPPING-VBCENTRE

museum, ______________________________

____

____

2 Stell dir vor, du triffst auf der Straße einen kleinen Mann vom Mars. Er braucht deine Hilfe. Was kannst du ihm sagen?

"I need some money."

"You can go to the ______________________ in Green Street."

"I want to send a letter to my parents."

"There is a ______________________ over there."

"I'd like to go by train."

"The ______________________ is in Station Road."

"I'm very hungry. Where can I get something to eat?"

"The ______________________ is in Main Street. It is very good."

"Wow, it's hot today!"

"You can go swimming at the ______________________ in Garden Street."

"Where can I find a room to sleep?"

"The ______________________ is in Elm Street. It is very nice."

"My English isn't very good. Where can I learn English?"

"There is a very good ______________________ in High Street."

"I'd like to go dancing."

"The ______________________ in Waterfront Road plays great music."

1 church, school, bookshop, hotel, post office, restaurant, department store, bank, supermarket, swimming pool, station, toy shop, disco, shopping centre

2 bank – post office – station – restaurant – swimming pool – hotel – school – disco

V 5/6

Das Datum von heute ____________

15 Aufbruch in den Urlaub (Verben)

Oje! Mr und Mrs Uptight fahren in den Urlaub. Sie fragen sich, ob sie auch wirklich an alles gedacht haben, bevor sie losfahren. Verbinde die Verben in dem Kreis mit den passenden Substantiven in dem Kasten und bilde Fragesätze. Für manche Wörter gibt es mehrere Möglichkeiten.

make
open
put
turn on
mow ✔
pay
close
lock
turn off
tidy up

the milkman
the cake in the cupboard
windows
the beds
the lights and the television
the grass ✔
the telephone answering machine
the cat's door
the kitchen
the front door

Darling, did you remember to mow the grass?

Darling, did you remember to ____________

____

____

____

____

____

____

____

Darling, did you remember to mow the grass?
Darling, did you remember to pay the milkman?
Darling, did you remember to tidy up the kitchen?
Darling, did you remember to turn on the telephone answering machine?
Darling, did you remember to open the cat's door?
Darling, did you remember to close the windows?
Darling, did you remember to make the beds?
Darling, did you remember to put the cake in the cupboard?
Darling, did you remember to lock the front door?

V
5/6

Das Datum von heute ___________

16 Briefeschreiber (Post)

1 Setze die fehlenden Wörter ein.

letter – stamps – Thank you – Dear – envelope – tell – Love – write – post office

__________ Colin,

_______________ for your _____________ . Of course I can _________ you about my hobbies. I'm good at football. I play in a club on Wednesdays and at the weekends. I like collecting _______________ , too. I put one on the _______________ for you. Every month I go to the ___________ ______________ because I buy the latest stamps there. Please _____________ back to me.

____________ , Johnny

2 Jenny ist im Postamt. Übersetze, was sie sagt. Hilfe findest du im Kasten rechts.

Here you are. – And I need a stamp for a postcard to the USA. – How much is it? – I have got a parcel to Italy. – I'd like to send this letter to Germany.

Man: Hello, can I help you, dear?

Jenny: Ich möchte diesen Brief nach Deutschland schicken. Wie viel kostet das?

____

____

Man: It's 35p.

Jenny: Und ich brauche eine Briefmarke für eine Postkarte in die USA.

____

Man: Here you are.

Jenny: Ich habe ein Paket nach Italien.

____

Man: Please fill in this form (Formular).

Jenny: Bitte schön. ____

Man: Good. That's £5.70, please. Thank you, here's your change.

1 Dear – Thank you – letter – tell – stamps – envelope – post office – write – Love

2 I'd like to send this letter to Germany. How much is it? – And I need a stamp for a postcard to the USA. – I have got a parcel to Italy. – Here you are.

V 5/6

Das Datum von heute __________

17 Schwarze Schafe (Wörterrätsel)

1 Black sheep: In jeder Reihe passt ein Wort nicht. Streiche es durch.

a aunt, sister, mother, father

b pen, biro, book, felt-tip

c bookshelf, dictionary, desk, chair

d morning, afternoon, evening, moment

e Wednesday, Thursday, Friday, January

f timetable, hour, minute, second

g street, bus, car, bike

h department store, supermarket, hotel, shopping centre

i station, road, airport, bus stop

j breakfast, apple juice, lunch, dinner

2 One is wrong: Ein Satz ist falsch. Streiche ihn durch.

a Your sister is your parents' child.
Your father and your mother are your parents.
My brother is my cousin's father.

b I can read a pencil.
I can draw with a felt-tip.
I can write with my pen.

c I can clean the board with a sponge.
The desk is on the cupboard.
I write on the board with a piece of chalk.

d An hour has got 24 days.
A minute is longer than a second.
A week has got seven days.

e Wednesday comes before Thursday.
Monday is the first day of the week.
Friday and Saturday are the weekend.

V 5/6

1 Black sheep:
a) father, b) book, c) dictionary, d) moment, e) January, f) timetable, g) street, h) hotel, i) road, j) apple juice

2 One is wrong:
a My brother is my cousin's father.
b I can read a pencil.
c The desk is on the cupboard.
d An hour has got 24 days.
e Friday and Saturday are the weekend.

Das Datum von heute ___________

18 Kopfnüsse knacken
(Wörter finden und zuordnen)

1 The fourth word: Finde das fehlende Wort.

a parents – teacher	children –	____________
b father – mother	brother –	____________
c day – night	today –	____________
d year – week	weeks –	____________
e one, two, three – 1, 2, 3 o'clock	numbers –	____________
f pen, ruler – pencil case	board, desk –	____________

2 Who says it and where?
Kreuze an, wer etwas sagt und wo es gesagt werden könnte.

	Customer	Assistant	Post office	Shop
I need a stamp for a letter to Italy.				
May I help you?				
I'm looking for a red pullover.				
What size do you need?				
This letter to England is 60p.				
Here is your change.				
How much is a parcel to the USA?				
Can I try it on?				

1 a) pupils, b) sister, c) tonight, d) days, e) time, f) class room

2

	Customer	Assistant	Post office	Shop
I need a stamp for a letter to Italy.	x		x	
May I help you?		x	x	x
I'm looking for a red pullover.	x			x
What size do you need?		x		x
This letter to England is 60p.		x	x	
Here is your change.		x	x	x
How much is a parcel to the USA?	x		x	
Can I try it on?	x			x

V 5/6

Das Datum von heute ___________

19 Das Fahrrad ist fort! (Schulweg)

1 Lies den Text. Wie oft findest du die Wörter *bike*, *school* und *snackbar* im Text?

odfJanetmkiskjfonerzherksjbike. Sheksdhashfjgotkeua helmetjfhgon. Shekal ways-jghtgoespiotokschoolkutbyg frbikemfbecausewhftherdgrschooltezishftwohgjdki-lom etresfgrhfromjhzrhome. Todaydgjfshejwegoeskgjtokfjasnackbarnmcbefor-ewezschool. “THerekjhyoufghare. That’slkj80pence.” Janetghutakesnbhermnsand-wichjkandkigoespuzoutgofertthemvnsnackbar. Shelkjg etswtza shockpkl. Wherep-nbiswdshertzgherbvcbike?

There are _____ *bikes*, _____ *schools*, and _____ *snackbars* in the text.

2 Hier kannst du die im Text versteckten Sätze noch einmal ordentlich aufschreiben.

____

____

____

____

____

____

____

____

____

____

____

____

____

1 There are 3 bikes, 3 schools and 2 snack bars.

1 Janet is on her bike. She has got a helmet on. She always goes to school by bike because her school is two kilometres from home.
Today she goes to a snack bar before school.
„Here you are. That’s 80 pence.“
Janet takes her sandwich and goes out of the snack bar.
She gets a shock. Where is her bike?

V 5/6

Das Datum von heute ___________

20 Im Wörterbuch (alphabetisch ordnen)

1 Finde den jeweils passenden Reimsatz.

a b c d e – ______________________

f g h i j k – ______________________

l m n o p q – ______________________

r s t u v – ______________________

w x y z – ______________________

I go to bed. I drink tea. And I say: I love you. I watch TV.

2 Welches Wort steht hier jeweils an der falschen Stelle?
Streiche es durch und zeichne einen Pfeil zur richtigen Stelle.

a		b		c		d	
	desk		hall		like		often
	dialogue		ham		litre		old
	dog		have		live		open
	dice		happy		letter		one
	dinner		hobby		look		order

3 Sortiere die Wörter alphabetisch.

assistant – board – cupboard – brother – afternoon – August – computer – boy

____

____

____

____

____

____

____

____

1 I drink tea. – And I say: – I love you. – I watch TV. – I go to bed.
2 a desk, dialogue, dice, dinner, dog b hall, ham, happy, have, hobby
c letter, like, litre, live, look d often, old, one, open, order
3 afternoon, assistant, August, board, boy, brother, computer, cupboard

Das Datum von heute ____________

21 Rund ums Haus (Gebäudeteile)

Verbinde jeweils das passende englische und deutsche Wort mit einer Linie.
Wörter, die du nicht kennst, schlägst du in deinem Wörterbuch nach.

In and around the house:

1	I	roof	17	I	Schornstein
2	I	attic	18	I	Treppen
3	E	chimney	19	R	Schubkarre
4	N	storeroom	20	L	Dach
5	B	stairs	21	H	Keller
6	G	cellar	22	V	Dachboden
7	O	study	23	R	Tor
8	S	hall	24	I	Bank
9	W	bench	25	E	Flur
10	T	hose	26	U	Arbeitszimmer
11	F	tree	27	S	Spaten
12	U	gate	28	E	Zaun
13	B	fence	29	H	Schlauch
14	D	wheelbarrow	30	A	Abstellraum
15	O	broom	31	O	Besen
16	M	spade	32	O	Baum

Nun kannst du den Satz entschlüsseln.
Trage dafür in die obere Zeile die Ziffern und in die untere die Buchstaben ein.

1	20																														
I	L																														

Mein Lösungssatz:

____

1	20	2	22	3	17	4	30	5	18	6	21	7	26	8	25	9	24	10	29	11	32	12	23	13	28	14	19	15	31	16	27
I	L	I	V	E	I	N	A	B	I	G	H	O	U	S	E	W	I	T	H	F	O	U	R	B	E	D	R	O	O	M	S

16	M	spade	32	O	Baum
15	O	broom	31	O	Besen
14	D	wheelbarrow	30	A	Abstellraum
13	B	fence	29	H	Schlauch
12	U	gate	28	E	Zaun
11	F	tree	27	S	Spaten
10	T	hose	26	U	Arbeitszimmer
9	W	bench	25	E	Flur
8	S	hall	24	I	Bank
7	O	study	23	R	Tor
6	G	cellar	22	V	Dachboden
5	B	stairs	21	H	Keller
4	N	storeroom	20	L	Dach
3	E	chimney	19	R	Schubkarre
2	I	attic	18	I	Treppen
1	I	roof	17	I	Schornstein

Das Datum von heute __________

22 Pizza und coke (Wörter sortieren)

1 eggs – cornflakes – orange juice – tomato salad – fish and chips – hamburger – sandwiches – bread – pizza – milk – marmalade – tea – apple juice – honey – coke

drinks	breakfast	lunch

2 Schreibe die folgenden Wörter in alphabetischer Reihenfolge in die richtigen Felder.

stationbaconcheeseairportshoppingcentregiraffeparrotbear
restaurantelephantchipsflatmeatbookshopsnackbarbread
penguindepartmentstoremonkeyjuicetomatotigerhamlion

animals	food	buildings

1 **drinks:** cola, apple juice, tea, milk, orange juice
breakfast: honey, bread, eggs, cornflakes, marmalade
lunch: fish and chips, pizza, hamburger, sandwiches, tomato salad

2 **animals:** bear, elephant, giraffe, lion, monkey, parrot, penguin, tiger
food: bacon, bread, cheese, chips, ham, juice, meat, tomato
buildings: airport, bookshop, department store, flat, restaurant, shopping centre, snack bar, station

V 5/6

Das Datum von heute ____________

23 Eine Menge Haustiere
(Wörter entschlüsseln)

Entziffere den Brief und schreibe auf, welche Tiere gemeint sind.

Dear Tom,

I want to tell you about my 

____

I have a  ______________. It lives in a cage. I feed it every day. Its name is Tweety. It can sing. And I have two  ____________. They can bark and run fast. Their names are Bob and Rover. My  ______________ sleep, eat and clean their faces all day. Their names are Ginger and Mog. They love eating  ______________.

My  ______________ lives in a cage, too. It sleeps all day and plays all night! Its name is Brownie. I have one brown , ____________, Sammy, and three white  ______________, Whitey, Micky and Stuart. They live in a cage in the garden house. Mum says that they smell. They eat cheese and bread.

Tweety is a ____________________.

Bob and Rover are ____________________.

Ginger and Mog are ____________________.

Brownie is a ____________________.

Sammy is a ____________________ ____________________.

Whitey, Mickey and Stuart are ____________________ ____________________.

V
5/6

animals, budgie, dogs, cats, fish, hamster, mouse, mice
budgie, dogs, cats, hamster, brown mouse, white mice

Das Datum von heute ____________

24 Wer wohnt hier? (logisch zuordnen)

2	4	6	8	10	12
			Paul		

Lies die Sätze unten gründlich durch und fülle dann die Tabelle aus.
Tipp: Beginne mit Bleistift zu schreiben. So kannst du leichter korrigieren.

Paul lives in number 8. ✔
Harry lives in number 10.
The goldfish lives in number 4.
Nancy lives beside Harry. Harry lives between the mouse and the dog.
The budgie lives beside Paul.
Carol lives between the white door and the blue door and she has a budgie.
Jill has a hamster.
Nancy has a yellow door and lives beside a green door.
The goldfish lives between the hamster and the budgie.
The dog lives in the house with a blue door.
Bill has a white door and lives between a red door and a brown door.
Paul lives between a red door and a cat.

No. 2 – Jill – hamster – brown
No. 4 – Bill – goldfish – white
No. 6 – Carol – budgie – red
No. 8 – Paul – dog – blue
No. 10 – Harry – cat – green
No. 12 – Nancy – mouse – yellow

Das Datum von heute ____________

25 Wer wird Millionär? (Präpositionen)

Ergänze in den Sätzen die fehlenden Wörter.

1 in, at, on

a "Who wants to be a millionaire?" is a programme ________ TV:

b What are you doing ________ the moment? – I'm doing my homework.

c What is 'Bügeleisen' ________ English?

d The post office is over there ________ the left.

e The postman is ________ the door with a parcel from Peter.

f You can see my brother ________ this photo. Look, he is standing beside me.

2 of, from, for

a We have school ________ Monday to Friday.

b Can I have a glass ________ milk please, mum?

c What is there ________ dinner, dad?

d This is a photo ________ our class. That's me in the front.

e I can pay ________ the ice-cream and you can pay ________ the cinema tickets.

f Where are you ________ ? – Germany.

g Let's wait ________ Betty after school.

3 on, out, at

a Look, that's Mr White, our English teacher, ________ the bus over there.

b Let's find ________ where Mr White is going.

c John is not ________ home, he is ________ with his friends.

d Don't sit ________ the table, sit ________ your chair.

e You can see the moon ________ night.

1 a) on, b) at, c) in, d) on, e) at, f) on
2 a) from, b) of, c) for, d) of, e) for – for, f) from, g) for
3 a) on, b) out, c) at – out, d) on – on , e) at

Das Datum von heute ___________

26 Kreuzworträtsel
(Verben und Präpositionen)

Löse dieses Kreuzworträtsel. Es handelt sich immer um ein Verb UND eine Präposition. Verwende für die Verben eine andere Farbe als für die Präpositionen.

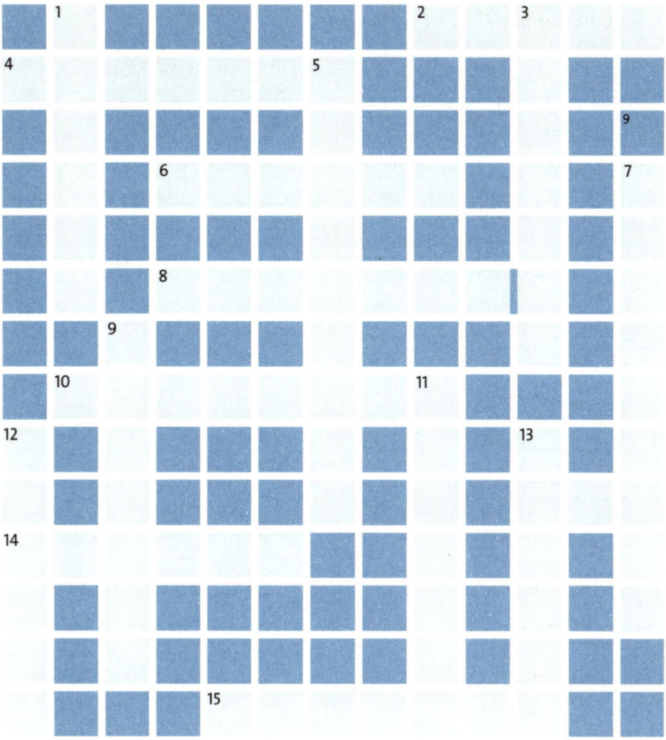

Across →

2 aufstehen
4 herausfinden
6 ausfüllen
8 träumen von
10 umherrennen
14 anschauen
15 warten auf

Down ↓

1 aufräumen
3 denken über
5 erzählen über
7 holen von
9 hinstellen
11 ausziehen
12 reden mit
13 bezahlen für

V
5/6

Das Datum von heute ____________

27 Was ist richtig? (Spiele und Hobbys)

Setze jeweils ein, was zutrifft.

alone	in summer and winter	in winter	?
in a team or group	in summer	with a partner	

a You can play chess with a partner in summer and winter.

b You can play volleyball and basketball ____________ ____________ in ____________.

c You can play football ____________ in ____________.

d You can do judo ____________ in ____________ ____________.

e You can play tennis ____________ in ____________.

f You can play ice hockey ____________ in ____________.

g In a drama club you work ____________. You can do it ____________.

h You collect stamps ____________, but you can show them to your friends all year round*, in ____________.

**all year round = das ganze Jahr über*

b) in a team or group – in summer and winter
c) in a team or group – in summer
d) with a partner – in summer and winter
e) with a partner – in summer
f) in a team or group – in winter
g) in a team or group – in summer and winter
h) alone – in summer and winter

28 Sonderangebot (Kleidung)

1 Lies dir die Anzeige durch und fertige eine Liste der Sommer- und der Winterkollektion an.

Special sale
Winter is over.
Forget your warm pair of jeans, scarf and pullover.
Our new summer collection is here:
Orange swimsuits and swimming trunks are great and cool for the summer.
Buy our latest shorts and T-shirts for only £ 5.95.
We still have got some warm shoes for a special price of only £ 15.75,
but what you really need is a new pair of sandals for only £ 18.90.
Our sweatshirts are ideal for a cool summer evening.

Summer collection	Winter collection

2 Was stimmt hier nicht? Schreibe auf, wie die Kleidungsstücke richtig heißen.

SWEAT	FORM	___________________
UNI	OVER	___________________
SWIM	SHIRT	___________________
PULL	SHIRT	___________________
T-	SUIT	___________________

1 Summer collection: swimsuit, swimming-trunks, shorts, T-shirts, sandals
Winter collection: jeans, scarf, pullover, warm shoes, sweatshirt
2 sweatshirt, uniform, swimsuit, pullover, T-shirt

29 Buchstabenschlange (Verben)

Übersetze das erste Verb. Finde die Buchstaben und kringle sie ein. Übrig bleibt das nächste deutsche Verb, dessen englische Übersetzung du im folgenden „Wort“ wieder einkringelst und so fort – bis zum Ende der Schlange.

SAGEN

W S O L A L E Y N → T W A A N N Z T E N

→ D G A U N C C K E E N → W W I A S S T E C H N

→ F L K I N E O G E W N → K A F U F L E Y N

→ B B E A N U T W O Y R T E N

→ S A A M M N E S L W E R N → C G O E L B L E E N C T

→ H G O L I E V E N → T F R A E G T E C H N

→ L W E E S A E R N → S C H R R E E A I D B E N

→ W L E R R I T N E E N → S C H L L E A A F R E N N

→ S S T L E E E H P E N → K S L T E A T T N E D R N

→ G C L L A A I M U B B E N → BELIEVE

sagen – say – wollen – want – tanzen – dance – gucken – watch – wissen – know – fliegen – fly – kaufen – buy – beantworten – answer – sammeln – collect – geben – give – holen – fetch – tragen – wear – lesen – read – schreiben – write – lernen – learn – schlafen – sleep – stehen – stand – klettern – climb – glauben – believe

Das Datum von heute __________

30 Kreuzworträtsel (Verben)

Löse das Kreuzworträtsel, indem du die Verben auf Englisch einträgst.

Across →

3 waschen
4 rennen, laufen
5 tragen, anziehen
7 zählen
10 träumen
11 fliegen
13 zusehen, sich anschauen, beobachten
15 lernen
16 tun, machen
17 geben
19 beantworten
21 öffnen
24 essen

Down ↓

1 benutzen, verwenden
2 trinken
3 schreiben
6 lesen, vorlesen
7 vervollständigen
8 sagen
9 wissen, kennen
11 finden
12 packen, einpacken
14 sauber machen, putzen
18 fragen, bitten
20 Fahrt
22 bezahlen
23 stellen, legen, tun

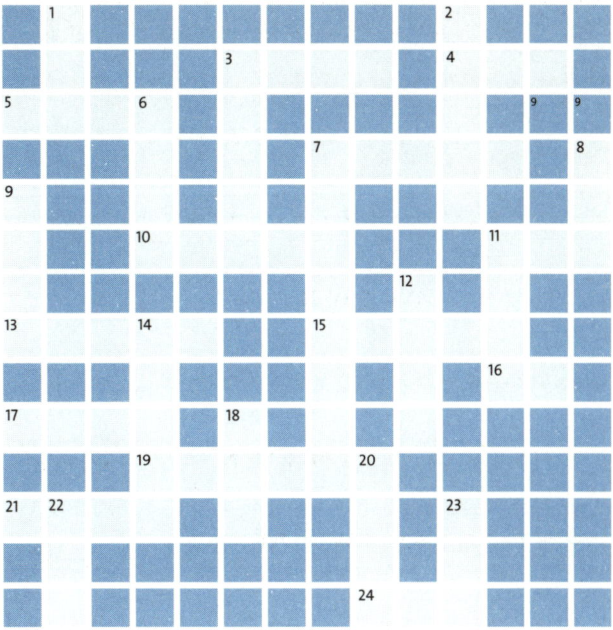

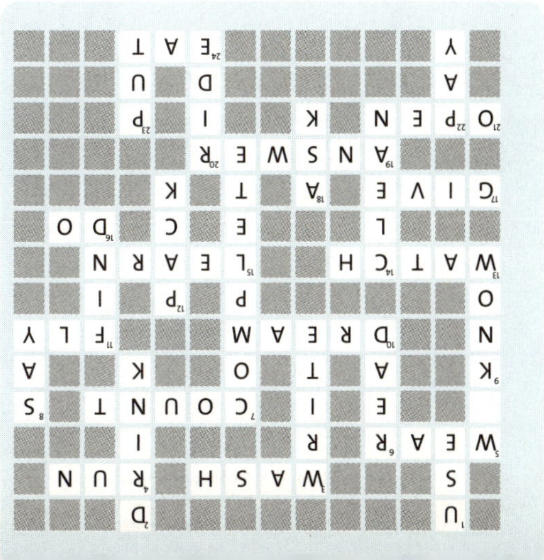

V
5/6

Das Datum von heute ____________

31 Eine Nachricht (Adjektive)

1 Nimm alle Adjektive aus diesem Satz heraus und du findest eine Nachricht!

Some old pupils stupid terrible clever copy late careful nice little bad new the right silly easy clean poor cool homework difficult good great cheap quiet from quick good their wrong happy friends dirty. Can small they learn big this expensive favourite way?

Der Lösungssatz lautet:

____

____

____

Deine Antwort:

____

2 Übersetze die Adjektive ins Deutsche. Benutze dazu das Wörterverzeichnis am Ende deines Lehrbuchs oder ein Wörterbuch.

old – alt, ______________________________

____

____

____

____

____

V 5/6

1 Some pupils copy the homework from their friends. Can they learn this way?
No, they can't.

2 stupid – dumm, terrible – furchtbar, clever – schlau, late – spät, careful – sorgfältig, nice – schön/hübsch, little – klein, new – neu, right – rechts/richtig, silly – albern/dumm, easy – leicht, clean – sauber, poor – arm, cool – kalt, difficult – schwierig, good – gut, great – groß(artig), cheap – billig, quiet – leise/still, quick – schnell, wrong – falsch, happy – glücklich, dirty – schmutzig, small – klein, big – groß, expensive – teuer, favourite – Lieblings-...

Das Datum von heute ___________

32 Stimmt genau! (Adjektive)

Verbinde die Gegensätze mit einem Lineal. Wenn du alles richtig hast, kannst du den Lösungssatz herausfinden.

1	bad	E	great
2	big	N	dark
3	clean	G	clever
4	difficult		wet
5	cheap	I	small
6	late	S R	good
7	hungry	H	thirsty
8	interesting	L	easy
9	happy		expensive
10	silly	G	dirty
11	dry	E I	boring
12	light	T S	early
13	cold	A	hot
14	terrible		sad

___ ___ ___ ___ ___ ___ ___   ___ ___   ___ ___ ___ ___ ___ !

1 2 3 4 5 6 7   8 9   10 11 12 13 14

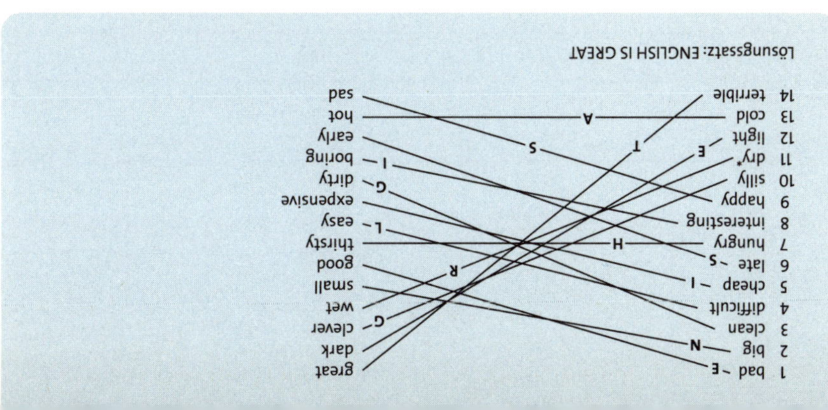

Das Datum von heute __________

33 Was kommt dahin?
(schwierige kleine Wörter)

1 Setze das richtige Wort ein: *of, from, at, on, in.*

a My birthday is ______ June.

b We don't go to school ______ the weekend.

c My mother is ______ America.

d I want a glass ______ milk, please.

e Here is a postcard ______ my father. He is in London at the moment.

f Peter isn't ______ school today. I think he is ______ home.

g I live ______ a flat ______ Green Street.

h Can you help me? Yes, ______ course.

2 **What can you …**

see in the house?	budgiefloorcupboardsongtabletrip
do in the afternoon?	playtheguitarmilkballrideabikeplaytennisswapstamps
buy?	magazinefilmflatmoneygoalday

Unterstreiche alle passenden Begriffe und schreibe sie richtig auf.

see in the house:

____

____

do in the afternoon:

____

____

buy: ____

V
5/6

1 a) in, b) at, c) in, d) of, e) from, f) at, at, g) in, in, h) of

2 *see in the house:* budgie, floor, cupboard, table
do in the afternoon: play the guitar, ride a bike, play tennis, swap stamps
buy: magazine, film, flat

Das Datum von heute ___________

34 Knack den Code! (Zahlen)

Hier ist die Tastatur eines Handys (auf Englisch *mobile phone*).
Die Zahlenkombination ergibt Wörter. Finde sie heraus.

1	2 ABC	3 DEF
4 GHI	5 JKL	6 MNO
7 PQRS	8 TUV	9 WXYZ
*	0 +	#

84373	273	2	568	63
________	________	________	________	________
9297	86	53276	3645474	288
________	________	________	________	________
93	4673	968	5453	8447
________	________	________	________	________
929				
________ !				

Überlege dir selbst einen englischen Satz und übertrage ihn in Handy-Zahlenkombinationen.

____

____

____

____

There are a lot of ways to learn English but we hope you like this way.

V 5/6

Das Datum von heute ____________

35 Als Aupair in Chicago (Tagesablauf)

Ruth arbeitet als Aupair für eine Familie in Chicago. Sie mag die Familie gut leiden, aber ihren Tagesablauf findet sie ziemlich anstrengend.
Ergänze alle fehlenden Wörter. Hier geht es um Dinge, die Ruth regelmäßig tut und nicht nur gerade jetzt, deswegen stehen die Verben, die du einsetzen sollst, im *simple present*.

~~his sister~~ – get up – girlfriend – wash – her husband – make – baby-sit – the wedding – take – mother – look after – cook

Dear Tim,

The family is very nice really. The kids are a lot of work but so cute. Johnny, the baby, is two and his sister [1] Mary is seven and in the first grade. The ________________ [2], Mrs Austin, works in a bank. She's single again because she and ______________________________ [3], Jerry, were divorced a year ago. He has a new ________________________ [4] now, and they love each other.

I think _____________________________ [5] will be in June.

My daily routine is not so easy. I __________________ [6] at 6.30 every morning and ____________ [7] breakfast for the family. Then I ______________ [8] Mary to school before Mrs Austin leaves for work at 8.30. When I come back I __________________ ____________ [9] Johnny, and try to do some housework. In the afternoon Johnny and I usually go to the park. Three evenings a week, I ___________________ [10] dinner. Then Mrs Austin and I ______________ [11] the dishes together.

What's your daily routine like these days? Do you still make tea for mum and dad every day at 5.00 ? And do you still ______________________ [12] the children next door at weekends?

Love

Ruth

V 5/6

1 his sister
2 mother
3 her husband
4 girlfriend
5 the wedding
6 get up
7 make
8 take
9 look after
10 cook
11 wash
12 baby-sit

Das Datum von heute ___________

36 Wo ist die Nase? (Körper)

1 Suche die 11 deutschen Körperwörter aus dem Buchstabenrätsel und übersetze sie so schnell wie möglich ins Englische. Suche waagerecht, senkrecht und auch diagonal!

Z	K	E	A	S	C	H	U	L	T	E	R	N
A	Ä	O	D	A	U	M	E	N	O	L	L	F
U	I	H	P	A	D	U	M	A	H	R	A	Ü
G	R	E	N	F	I	N	G	E	R	T	A	S
E	S	T	C	E	K	D	Z	X	E	B	J	S
N	W	G	E	S	I	C	H	T	N	A	S	E

2 Dann setze die englischen Wörter in den Lückentext ein.

1 I have four ______________ and one ______________ on each hand.

2 Your neck is between your ______________ and your ______________ .

3 My ______________ is in the middle of my face.

4 Her ______________ are inside her mouth.

5 Your ______________ are at the end of your legs.

6 His nose is under his ______________ and above his mouth.

7 Her eyes, nose and ______________ are all part of her ______________ .

8 Your ______________ are on the side of your head.

1 Schultern – shoulders
Daumen – thumb
Zähne – teeth
Füße – feet
Nase – nose
Gesicht – face
Augen – eyes
Kopf – head
Finger – finger
Mund – mouth
Ohren – ears

2 1 fingers – thumb
2 head – shoulders
3 nose
4 teeth
5 feet
6 eyes
7 mouth – face
8 ears

Das Datum von heute ____________

37 Kleider machen Leute (Kleidung)

Löse das Kleidungs-Worträtsel. Wie lautet das Lösungswort?

1 People wear these on their feet.
2 Men wear them at the beach and in the sea.
3 They are usually blue, very popular and come from the States.
4 A lot of people wear one in winter, on top of all the other clothes.
5 A short version of number four.
6 Another word for number 3 above.
7 Usually men wear a tie with it.
8 It's more than just a bikini.
9 Women and Scottish men wear one.
10 Trousers with short legs.

Lösungswort:

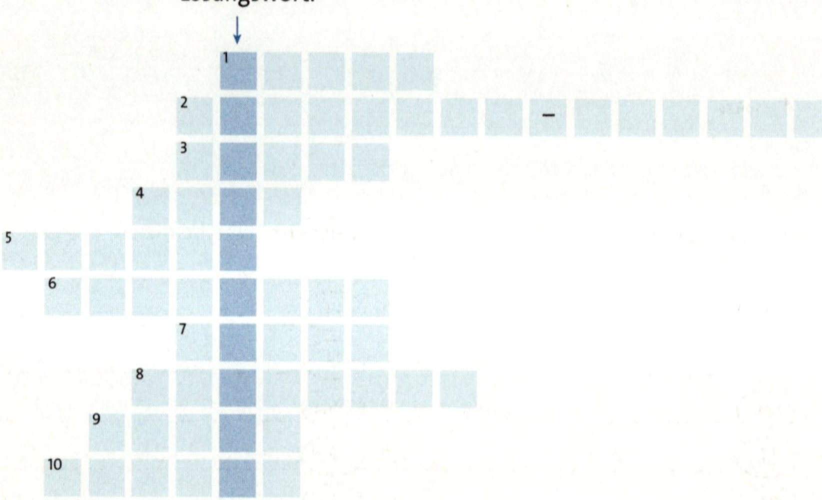

1 shoes
2 swimming-trunks
3 jeans
4 coat
5 jacket
6 trousers
7 shirt
8 swimsuit
9 skirt
10 shorts

Lösungswort: sweatshirt

V
5/6

Das Datum von heute ___________

38 Viel unterwegs (Länder und Verkehr)

1 Ordne die folgenden Wörter den drei Begriffen Luft, Land und Wasser zu.

~~helicopter~~ – flight – station – tanker – to drive – steering wheel – to fly – bus tour – by car – airline – to ride a bike – caravan – traffic jam – to park – by plane – ship – to take off – by bus – bus stop – by ferry – ambulance – garage – airport – to land – by coach – underground – port – traffic lights – motorway – by train

Luft:	helicopter
Land:	
Wasser:	

2 Aus welchen Ländern kommen diese Autokennzeichen? Schreibe die englischen Namen auf.

1	CH	Switzerland	9	H	___________
2	L	___________	10	D	___________
3	IRL	___________	11	USA	___________
4	PL	___________	12	F	___________
5	FIN	___________	13	E	___________
6	SLO	___________	14	TR	___________
7	A	___________	15	GB	___________
8	N	___________	16	NL	___________

1 **Luft:** helicopter, flight, to fly, airline, by plane, to take off, airport, to land.
Land: station, to drive, steering wheel, bus tour, by car, to ride a bike, caravan, traffic jam, to park, by bus, bus stop, ambulance, garage, by coach, underground, traffic lights, motorway, by train.
Wasser: tanker, ship, by ferry, port.

2

1 Switzerland	5 Finland	9 Hungary	13 Spain
2 Luxembourg	6 Slovakia	10 Germany	14 Turkey
3 Ireland	7 Austria	11 United States	15 Great Britain
4 Poland	8 Norway	12 France	16 the Netherlands

Das Datum von heute __________

39 Wo geht's lang? (Wegbeschreibung)

Hier sind einige wichtige Wörter, die man braucht, um Wege zu beschreiben. Übersetze, was in den Klammern steht. Manchmal musst du mehrere Wörter einfügen.

1 Every morning I walk (entlang) along the street to the bus stop.

2 He leaves his dog (draußen vor) __________ the supermarket when he goes shopping.

3 You'll find the pub (zwischen) __________ Oxford Street and College Street.

4 She always waits for me (vor) __________ the library.

5 We often swim in the lake (hinter) __________ the park.

6 Then we eat lunch in the pub (gegenüber) __________ the church.

7 Shall we go to the new restaurant (in der Nähe von) __________ the shopping centre?

8 The London Hotel? Oh, it's (nicht weit) __________ from here at all.

9 She is driving as fast as she can (in Richtung) __________ __________ the hospital.

10 Walk (an … vorbei) __________ the museum and take the first left. You can't miss it.

11 They both work in an office (neben) __________ to the central station.

1 along
2 outside
3 between
4 in front of
5 behind
6 opposite
7 near the
8 not far
9 in the direction of
10 past
11 next

V 5/6

Das Datum von heute __________

40 Noahs Arche (Tiere)

Welche der folgenden Tiere müssen in welchen Teil von Noahs Arche? Schreibe die englischen Namen der Tiere in die richtige Abteilung. Manchmal gibt es mehrere Möglichkeiten.

~~Schwein~~ – Pferd – Tiger – Hund – Vogel – Hamster – Schaf – Katze – Schlange – Eisbär – Kuh – Schildkröte – Elefant – Wolf – Gorilla – Gans – Nilpferd – Bär – Pinguin – Ente – Känguru – Seelöwe – Huhn – Giraffe – Maus – Papagei – Hahn – Kaninchen – Goldfisch

Farm animals only:

pig, ____

____

____

Zoo animals only:

____

____

____

Pets only:

____

____

____

Farm animals only
Pig, horse, dog, bird, sheep, cat, cow, goose, duck, chicken/hen, mouse, cockerel, rabbit.
Zoo animals only
Tiger, snake, polar bear, elephant, wolf, gorilla, hippopotamus, bear, penguin, kangaroo, seal, giraffe, parrot, tortoise.
Pets only
Dog, bird, hamster, cat, tortoise, mouse, parrot, rabbit, goldfish.

41 Urlaubsgrüße (Urlaub)

1 Vicky macht mit ihrer Familie in Cornwall Urlaub. Sie schreibt einen Brief an ihre deutsche Brieffreundin Greta. Ergänze den Brief mit den Wörtern und Ausdrücken.

beaches – hills – village – farmhouse – go hiking – on the coast – river – on the beach – path – sand

Dear Greta,

We're staying in a two-hundred-years-old ______________ [1] with a big garden and behind the house is a ______________ [2] where you can go fishing. The house is near a ______________ [3] with shops and a pub. Cornwall is perfect for swimming – our house is ______________ [4] so you can spend every day in the sun ______________ [5] if you want. There's a small ______________ [6] which goes from the house straight down to the sea – you can walk there in five minutes. The water is clean and there are beautiful ______________ [7] with white ______________ [8] everywhere. There are lots of high ______________ [9] and moors in Cornwall where you can ____________________ [10] or sleep in a tent. North Cornwall is very beautiful and I really like it here.

Love Vicky

2 Was passt wozu? Verbinde die Verben mit den dazu passenden Nomen.

to milk
to mow
to put up
to ride
to visit
to take ... for a walk

the grass
a tent
a pony
a cow
a dog
a safari park

V 5/6

1 1 farmhouse
2 river
3 village
4 on the coast
5 on the beach
6 path
7 beaches
8 sand
9 hills
10 go hiking

2 to mow the grass
to put up a tent
to milk a cow
to ride a pony
to take a dog for a walk
to visit a safari park

Das Datum von heute ____________

42 Essen Elefanten Schokolade?
(Tiere)

Silly questions. Schau dir die Beispielsätze an und bilde die richtigen Fragen und Antworten.

Elephants / eat / chocolate?

Do elephants eat chocolate? No, they don't.

Hamsters / be / popular as pets?

Are hamsters popular as pets? Yes, of course they are.

1 Hippos / use / soap?

____

2 Tigers / eat / meat?

____

3 Parrots / do / homework?

____

4 Kangaroos / write / letters?

____

5 Giraffes / be / bigger/ than mice?

____

6 Wolves / be / dangerous?

____

7 Penguins / go / to school?

____

8 Birds / live / in the ocean?

____

1 Do hippos use soap? No, they don't.
2 Do tigers eat meat? Yes, of course they do.
3 Do parrots do homework? No, they don't.
4 Do kangaroos write letters? No, they don't.
5 Are giraffes bigger than mice? Yes, of course they are.
6 Are wolves dangerous? Yes, of course they are.
7 Do penguins go to school? No, they don't.
8 Do birds live in the ocean? No, they don't.

Das Datum von heute ____________

43 Vom Essen und Trinken
(Lebensmittel)

1 Das Schiff von Mr Robinson Cruise ist gesunken und er konnte sich auf eine einsame Insel retten. Jede Nacht träumt er jetzt vom Essen, weil er so hungrig und so durstig ist. Die Wörter sind in seinem Traum etwas durcheinandergeraten. Bringe die Buchstaben in die richtige Reihenfolge.

1 aotts ____________	10 newi ____________
2 mah ____________	11 erbe ____________
3 crema ____________	12 urtetb ____________
4 zapiz ____________	13 tekphcu ____________
5 fihsandhcips ____________	14 sitpehgat ____________
6 oprncpo ____________	15 ragus ____________
7 ajm ____________	16 peatuns ____________
8 oyghurt ____________	17 hceees
9 ffeeoc ____________	18 swtees ____________

2 Was passt hier zusammen? Verbinde die richtigen Paare.

to bake, to open, orange, salt, ice, fish, cup, to boil, toast, knife, baked, to fry, tea, bread

and pepper, cream, and chips, an egg, and marmalade, juice, with milk and sugar, a can, and butter, some bacon, and saucer, beans, and fork, a cake

3 Welche Dinge aus der Liste oben würde ein Vegetarier nie essen? Unterstreiche sie.

1 1 toast	10 wine	**2** salt and pepper	tea with milk and sugar
2 ham	11 beer	to bake a cake	to open a can
3 cream	12 butter	ice cream	knife and fork
4 pizza	13 ketchup	fish and chips	cup and saucer
5 fish and chips	14 spaghetti	orange juice	toast and marmalade
6 popcorn	15 sugar	baked beans	
7 jam	16 peanuts	bread and butter	**3** Vegetarier:
8 yoghurt	17 cheese	to boil an egg	fish and bacon
9 coffee	18 sweets	to fry some bacon	

V 5/6

Das Datum von heute ___________

44 Scheine und Münzen (Geld)

Ergänze die acht englischen „Geldwörter“: coin, pocket money, note, sell, save, price, spend, cheque.

1 It’s small, it’s made of metal, and you use it to pay for things. ______________

2 It’s bigger than number 1 above,
it’s made of paper, and you also use it to pay for things. ______________

3 The money you get from your
parents every week or every month (you hope!). ______________

4 What something costs. ______________

5 The opposite of ‘buy’. ______________

6 What people in Scotland like to do with their money (a verb). ______________

7 The opposite of number 6 above (also a verb). ______________

8 A piece of paper printed by a bank that you can fill in, and use to pay for things.
____

1 coin
2 note
3 pocket money
4 price
5 sell
6 save
7 spend
8 cheque

V 5/6

Das Datum von heute ____________

45 Ein Kinderspiel? (Verben)

Ergänze den Text mit der passenden Verbform.

1 We (go) ___went___ shopping yesterday.

2 Has she (make) ___made___ the tea yet?

3 Look, I've (cut) ___cut___ the meat for you.

4 Judy has already (buy) ___bought___ some vegetables.

5 What did they (sell) ___sell___ you in the boutique?

6 He (pay) ___paid___ almost £200 for a coat a year ago.

7 She's (drink) ___drunk___ all the mineral water.

8 I (prepare) ___prepared___ the meal last night.

9 Have you (keep) ___kept___ it in the fridge all day?

10 How much did the eggs (cost) ___cost___

11 They (be) ___were___ for sale in the supermarket last week.

12 Have you (be) ___been___ to the new computer shop yet?

Jetzt füge die Verbformen von oben ein. Verwende die unterlegten Buchstaben und setze das Lösungswort zusammen.

It looks like something you can eat, but in fact it means in English "Es ist ein Kinderspiel".

It's a piece of A B C D .

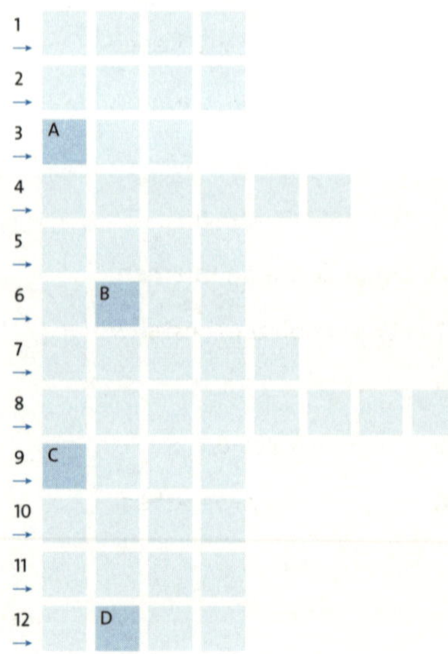

1 went	5 sell	9 kept	Lösungswort: cake
2 made	6 paid	10 cost	
3 cut	7 drunk	11 were	
4 bought	8 prepared	12 been	

Das Datum von heute ___________

46 Auf einer Party (Konversation)

1 Was sagen die Jugendlichen auf der Party zueinander? Verbinde die Sätze 1–9 mit den passenden Antworten a–i.

1 Sorry I'm late. I missed the bus. ○

2 This is Sue. May I speak to Jim? ○

3 Oh Cindy. This is my brother Mike. ○

4 Could you show me how to do this dance, please? ○

a Sorry he isn't home. Can I take a message?
b Hi Cindy. Nice to meet you.
c I'd like a coke, please. ✔
d It's great. But a little too loud.
e Of course. I'll be glad to.
f I'm fine, thank you, and you?
g Oh thanks, I'm really hungry.
h Oh yes, I'd love to. That's a great song.
i That's all right. Don't worry.

5 Would you like something to drink? (c)

6 Would you like to dance? ○

7 How do you like the music? ○

8 Hello, how are you this evening? ○

9 Here you are! ○

2 Oben findest du Beispiele für die folgenden Gesprächssituationen. Ordne sie zu.

1 Begrüßung Hello, how are you this evening?
2 nach der Meinung fragen ____________________
3 eine Meinung äußern ____________________
4 jemanden vorstellen ____________________
5 sich entschuldigen ____________________
6 jemanden kennenlernen ____________________
7 etwas anbieten/bestellen ____________________
8 telefonieren ____________________
9 um etwas bitten ____________________
10 jemandem etwas geben ____________________

1 1i **2** 1 Hello, how are you this evening?
2a 2 How do you like the music?
3b 3 It's great but a little too loud.
4e 4 This is my brother Mike.
5c 5 Sorry, I'm late.
6h 6 Hi Mike, nice to meet you.
7d 7 Would you like something to drink?
8f 8 This is Sue. May I speak to Jim?
9g 9 Could you show me how to do this dance?
10 Here you are.

V 5/6

Das Datum von heute ____________

47 Sehr sportlich! (Sport)

1 Hier sind 10 verschiedene Sportarten. Kannst du die Buchstaben in die richtige Reihenfolge bringen?

1 huasqs	**2** nixbog	**3** djuo	**4** kochye	**5** inunrng

1 ____________ **6** ____________

2 ____________ **7** ____________

3 ____________ **8** ____________

4 ____________ **9** ____________

5 ____________ **10** ____________

6 itkrcec	**7** akgniyka	**8** valbelyoll	**9** isnwbaogondr	**10** blnicmig

2 Wenn du die richtigen Wörter der beiden Gruppen verbindest, bekommst du eine Sportart. Manchmal brauchst du einen Bindestrich! Wenn du dir nicht sicher bist, schaue die Schreibweise in deinem Wörterbuch nach.

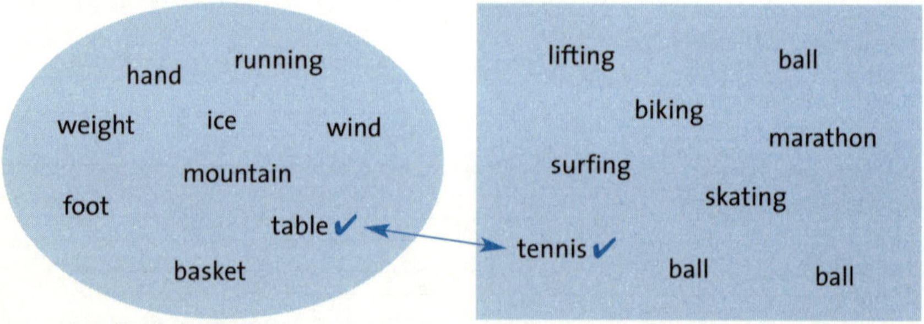

1 table tennis

2 ____________ **6** ____________

3 ____________ **7** ____________

4 ____________ **8** ____________

5 ____________ **9** ____________

V 5/6

1 1 squash 2 boxing 3 judo 4 hockey 5 running 6 cricket 7 kayaking 8 volleyball 9 snowboarding 10 climbing
2 1 table tennis 2 ice-skating 3 basketball 4 mountain-biking 5 weightlifting 6 windsurfing 7 handball 8 marathon-running 9 football

Das Datum von heute __________

48 Gut im Sport? (Sport)

Hier ist die Geschichte von Jane und ihren Erfahrungen mit Sport.
Die Sätze sind nicht in der richtigen Reihenfolge. Benutze die deutschen Hinweise, um die Sätze in die richtige Reihenfolge zu bringen.

1 nie gut im Sport
2 hat immer Hockey gehasst
3 zu klein für Basketball
4 Unfall gehabt
5 schaut sich Tennis im Fernsehen an

- She went skiing at Christmas, had an accident and broke her leg. Poor Jane!
- She played basketball with some friends in the summer holidays, but she was too short to be good at it.
- She decided that winter sports were too dangerous, so she watched the tennis on TV instead!
- At school she always hated hockey and she was too lazy to enjoy running.
- Jane has never been good at sport.

____
____
____
____
____
____
____
____
____
____
____
____
____
____
____
____
____
____

1 Jane has never been good at sport.
2 At school she always hated hockey and she was too lazy to enjoy running.
3 She played basketball with some friends in the summer holidays, but she was too short to be good at it.
4 She went skiing at Christmas, had an accident and broke her leg. Poor Jane!
5 She decided that winter sports were too dangerous, so she watched the tennis on TV instead!

Das Datum von heute ____________

49 Klarer Himmel (Wetter)

1 Letzte Woche war das Wetter wirklich fantastisch, diese Woche ist es ganz schlecht. Der Wetterbericht von letzter Woche wurde mit dem von dieser Woche zusammengeworfen. Streiche alle falschen Begriffe von letzter Woche durch.

"Good morning. Here's the weather forecast. There's going to be **sun and rain**[1] every day this week in the South, I'm afraid, with **some light wind and some very strong wind**[2] on the coast. In Cornwall there will be **clear skys with bad storms and clouds everywhere**[3], and in the mornings we'll have **low temperatures with high temperatures**[4]. So the week in most of the country will be **hot and dry, but also wet and cold**[5].
In the North a new **cold, warm front**[6] is coming from the Atlantic and is bringing **lots of fog and snow and hot weather**[7] with it. The evenings will be extremely **cool and warm**[8]. And that's ... um ... ah ...the end of the weather forecast. Goodbye."

2 Wie ist das Wetter heute? Ergänze den Text mit den passenden Adjektiven.

foggy – rainy – snowy – windy – sunny

1 What a ____________ day! Shall we go to the beach?

2 It's very ____________ today, the washing is dry already.

3 Don't forget your umbrella – it's very ____________ outside.

4 Don't ride your bike today! It's so ____________ you can't see anything.

5 Is it ____________ outside? – Yes, you'll need your hat and gloves.

V
5/6

1 1 rain
2 some very strong wind
3 bad storms and clouds everywhere
4 low temperatures
5 wet and cold
6 cold front
7 lots of fog and snow
8 cool

2 1 sunny
2 windy
3 rainy
4 foggy
5 snowy

Das Datum von heute ____________

50 Sport und Spiel (Quiz)

Wie viele Fragen über Sport und Spiel kannst du beantworten?
Kreuze die richtigen Antworten an.

1 The youngest person to win Wimbledon was …
- ◯ **a** Martina Hingis
- ◯ **b** Andre Agassi
- ◯ **c** Steffi Graf
- ◯ **d** Boris Becker

2 The first marathon was
- ◯ **a** 2500 years ago
- ◯ **b** 600 years ago
- ◯ **c** 100 years ago
- ◯ **d** 59 years ago

3 In 1996, which country won the European Championship in football?
- ◯ **a** Norway
- ◯ **b** Czech Republic
- ◯ **c** Germany
- ◯ **d** England

4 How many people are on a football team?
- ◯ **a** 9
- ◯ **b** 10
- ◯ **c** 11
- ◯ **d** 12

5 Which football team plays in England?
- ◯ **a** Tottenham Hotspurs
- ◯ **b** Glasgow Rangers
- ◯ **c** Dynamo Kiev
- ◯ **d** Ajax Amsterdam

6 What is the name of the city where the Olympic games were held in 2004?
- ◯ **a** Atlanta
- ◯ **b** Paris
- ◯ **c** Berlin
- ◯ **d** Athens

7 In what country were the Olympics first held?
- ◯ **a** Egypt
- ◯ **b** Ireland
- ◯ **c** Greece
- ◯ **d** Nepal

8 What famous mountains are in Nepal?
- ◯ **a** The Himalayas
- ◯ **b** The Rockies
- ◯ **c** The Alps
- ◯ **d** The Urals

9 The first person to climb Mount Everest was …
- ◯ **a** Reinhold Messner in 1980
- ◯ **b** Sylvester Stallone in 1977
- ◯ **c** Terry Swartzberg in 1982
- ◯ **d** Edmund Hillary in 1953

10 Sylvester Stallone played an athlete in the film 'Rocky'. Rocky was a …
- ◯ **a** skater
- ◯ **b** boxer
- ◯ **c** mountain climber
- ◯ **d** table tennis player

1 Boris Becker
2 2500 years ago
3 Germany
4 11
5 Tottenham Hotspurs
6 Athens
7 Greece
8 The Himalayas
9 Edmund Hillary in 1953
10 boxer

Das Datum von heute ___________

51 Der regelmäßige Plural

Bilde den Plural der unten angegebenen Substantive.

1 At school

chair	________	class	________
desk	________	felt-tip	________
girl	________	lesson	________
pen	________	pencil	________
shelf	________	table	________

2 Clothes

blouse	________	coat	________
dress	________	jacket	________
pullover	________	shoe	________

3 Food and drink

apple	________	cake	________
drink	________	potato	________
sausage	________	biscuit	________
cheese	________	orange	________
sandwich	________	tomato	________

4 Transport

bicycle	________	car	________
plane	________	taxi	________
van	________	bus	________
lorry	________	ship	________
train	________	wheel	________

G 5/6

1 chairs – classes – desks – felt-tips – girls – lessons – pens – pencils – shelves – tables
2 blouses – coats – dresses – jackets – pullovers – shoes
3 apples – cakes – drinks – potatoes – sausages – biscuits – cheeses – oranges – sandwiches – tomatoes
4 bicycles – cars – planes – taxis – vans – buses – lorries – ships – trains – wheels

Das Datum von heute __________

52 Der unregelmäßige Plural

Setze die angegebenen Substantive in den Text ein.
Pass dabei gut auf, weil einige davon in der Einzahl bleiben müssen.

The __________ (child) of Miss Jolly's __________ (form) are very excited. They are having a form __________ (party), and they think that __________ (party) are great. Miss Jolly is talking to the __________ (boy) and __________ (girl) about everything they must do. 'What about __________ (knife) and __________ (fork)?' she says. 'And who can bring some __________ (cup) and __________ (glass)?' 'I can,' says Sally. Miss Jolly writes down Sally's __________ (name) on one of her __________ (list).

'Now,' she goes on, 'let's talk about the __________ (food). What should we have?' 'Oh,' says Freddy, 'lots of lovely cream __________ (biscuit), chocolate __________ (cake) and __________ (toffee), of course, Miss.' 'Don't be a silly __________ (boy), Freddy,' says Miss Jolly. 'Sweet __________ (thing) are very bad for your __________ (tooth).'

G 5/6

children – form – party – parties – boys – girls – knives – forks – cups – glasses – name – lists – food – biscuits – cake – toffees – boy – things – teeth

Das Datum von heute ___________

53 Der 's- und of-Genitiv

Übersetze die unterstrichenen Teile der Sätze ins Englische.

1 Die Kinder spielen oft in Cobbs Garten.

____

2 Sallys Hund,Spooky, und Mrs Cobbs Vogel, Tweets, mögen gern Schokolade.

____

____

____

3 Mr Pratt muss das Fenster von Bobs Zimmer streichen.

____

____

4 Freddys Haus ist am Ende der Straße gegenüber der Bäckerei.

____

____

5 Toms Mathebuch ist dreckig und sechs Seiten des Buches fehlen.

____

____

6 Mrs Nunn ist krank. Sie muss zum Arzt gehen.

____

____

7 Der Ärmel *(sleeve)* von Elviras Discokleid ist kaputt.

____

____

G 5/6

1 in the Cobb's garden
2 Sally's dog – Mrs Cobb's bird
3 the window of Bob's room
4 Freddy's house – at the end of the street
5 Tom's maths book – six pages of the book
6 to the doctor's
7 the sleeve of Elvira's disco dress

Das Datum von heute __________

54 Der bestimmte Artikel the

1 Unterstreiche den bestimmten Artikel, bei dem du das **e** wie das **ie** in ‚Liebe' aussprechen musst [di:].

the airport; the aunt; the bottle; the cat; the CD; the engineer; the English book; the exercise; the flower; the garden; the hospital; the house; the ice-cream; the invitation; the jeans; the new school; the old town; the record player; the taxi-driver; the uncle.

2 Setze den bestimmten Artikel nur dann ein, wenn es nötig ist.

1 Elvira doesn't live in ________ Oak Lane. She lives in ___the___ white house at ________ end of ________ Cherry Tree Road.

2 ________ most/Most of ________ boys at ________ Green Park School like football, but a lot of ________ girls think that ________ basketball or ________ jazz dance is more fun.

3 – Do you go to ________ school by ________ bus or by ________ train?
– Well, I go by ________ taxi, actually. ________ taxi/Taxi beiongs to my dad, you see.

4 – Should we go to ________ town today? ________ film/Film about the Eskimos is on at ________ cinema in ________ Station Road.
– Yes, OK. We can go by ________ bike, can't we?

1 (the airport) – the aunt – the engineer – the English book – the exercise – the ice-cream – the invitation – the old town – the uncle

2 1 Elvira doesn't live in Oak Lane, she lives in the white house at the end of Cherry Tree Road.
2 Most of the boys at Green Park School like football, but a lot of the girls think that basketball or jazz dance is more fun.
3 – Do yout go to school by bus or by train?
– Well, I go by taxi, actually. The taxi belongs to my dad, you see.
4 – Should we go to town today? The film about the Eskimos is on at the cinema in Station Road.
– Yes, OK. We can go by bike, can't we?

G 5/6

Das Datum von heute ____________

55 Der unbestimmte Artikel a/an

Übersetze die unterstrichenen Teile der Sätze ins Englische.

1 Miss Jolly ist Lehrerin.

____

2 Bob hat Kopfschmerzen und Freddy hat Zahnschmerzen.

____

3 Tom ist so langsam. Wir sind in Eile.

____

4 Die Kinder machen Lärm, wenn der Lehrer zu spät kommt.

____

5 Wir müssen immer lange Zeit auf den Bus warten.

____

6 Elvira hat eine Uniform, aber sie zieht sie nie an.

____

7 Mr Pratt ist krank. Er hat Bauchschmerzen.

____

8 Wie schade! Der Fernseher ist kaputt.

____

9 Tom duscht sich gerade.

____

10 Sally will Krankenschwester werden, wenn sie groß ist.

____

G 5/6

1 is a teacher
2 has (got) a headache – has (got) toothache
3 in a hurry
4 make a noise
5 for a long time
6 has (got) a uniform
7 has got stomache ache
8 What a pity!
9 is having a shower
10 wants to become a nurse

Das Datum von heute __________

56 Die Pronomen

1 Ersetze alle Namen mit Pronomen in der Subjektform. Trage die Pronomen rechts ein.

1 Tom goes to school by bike. ___he___
2 Sally eats cornflakes for breakfast. ________
3 Elvira has got some new dancing shoes. ________
4 The Opel is standing in front of the house. ________
5 Bob, Tom and Freddy all live in Oak Lane. ________
6 Miss Jolly teaches in Kingston. ________
7 Fiats and Lancias are cars from Italy. ________

2 Ersetze alle Namen mit Pronomen in der Objektform. Trage die Pronomen rechts ein.

1 We all like Miss Jolly. ___her___
2 The dog ran after Freddy. ________
3 My mother went to see Mr and Mrs Pratt yesterday. ________
4 The boys watched Elvira and Sally playing basketball. ________
5 The policeman stopped the BMW in King Street. ________
6 Bob gave Sally a box of chocolates. ________
7 Mr Carter teaches the boys and girls well. ________

1 2 she
3 she
4 it
5 they
6 she
7 they

2 2 him
3 them
4 them
5 it
6 her
7 them

G
5/6

57 Fehlende Pronomen

Trage die fehlenden Pronomen sowohl in der Subjektform als auch in der Objektform ein.

Yesterday my mother saw the girls. __________[1] were in the shop.

My mother talked to __________[2].

__________[3] told __________[4] that __________[5] were looking for a present for Freddy. But __________[6] didn't know what to buy __________[7]. My mother said __________[8] should buy a CD for __________[9], but the girls said __________[10] didn't want to buy a disc. __________[11] thought __________[12] was too expensive. Sally said __________[13] thought that a book was a good idea but Elvira thought __________[14] was a silly idea. __________[15] said Freddy already had a book, and __________[16] didn't like __________[17]. Suddenly Freddy came into the shop. '__________[18] know that __________[19] are talking about __________[20]', __________[21] said. '__________[22] don't know what to buy for my birthday. Well, __________[23] want lots of toffees for my birthday. __________[24] know how much __________[25] love __________[26].'

1 they, 2 them, 3 They, 4 her, 5 they, 6 they, 7 him, 8 they, 9 him, 10 they, 11 They, 12 it, 13 she, 14 it, 15 She, 16 he, 17 it, 18 I, 19 you, 20 me, 21 he, 22 You, 23 I, 24 You, 25 I, 26 them

Das Datum von heute ____________

58 Die possessive pronouns I

Übersetze die unterstrichenen Teile der Sätze ins Englische.

1 Bob bekam einen Fußball zu *(for)* seinem Geburtstag.

____

Seine Schwester gab ihm ein Buch.

____

2 Mrs Nunn räumt ihren Bus jeden Abend auf.

____

3 Freddy versteckt seine Toffees unter seinem Schreibtisch.

____

Sie liegen auf seinem Englischbuch.

____

4 Der arme Vogel hat sich den Flügel *(wing)* gebrochen.

____

5 Die kleinen Kinder tragen ihre Schultaschen auf dem Rücken *(back)*, da sie sehr schwer sind.

____

____

6 Elvira hat ihre Tanzschuhe vergessen.

____

1 for his birthday – his sister
2 her bus
3 his toffees – his desk – his English book
4 its wing
5 their school bags – their back
6 her dancing shoes

Das Datum von heute __________

59 Die possessive pronouns II

Bill, Will und Jill sind sehr unordentliche Drillinge. Um ihre Sachen auseinanderzuhalten, hat die Mutter alles mit Buchstaben versehen. Die Eltern wollen aufräumen, aber der Vater weiß nicht, wem die Dinge gehören.

Vater Is this Bill's?
Mutter No, it's not his. It's Will's.

1 Is this Jill's comic?

No, it's not ______________ . It's ______________ .

2 Is this Will's record?

No, it's not ______________ . It's ______________ .

3 Is this Bill's shoe?

No, it's not ______________ . It's ______________ .

4 Is this the boys' football?

Yes, it is ______________ .

5 Is this Bill's tennis ball?

No, it's not ______________ . It's ______________ .

6 Is this Bill's school-bag?

____

7 Is this Bill's radio?

____

1 hers – Bill's
2 his – Bill's
3 his – Will's
4 theirs
5 his – Jill's
6 No, it's not his. It's Jill's.
7 No, it's not his. It's mine.

Das Datum von heute ___________

60 Die Demonstrativpronomen

Setze ein Demonstrativpronomen ein.

1 – Is __this__ your dog here?

– No, __that__ is my dog over there.

2 – Who is ________ man over there?

– Which man? Oh, ________ man. ________ is Mr Carter.

3 Which shoes do you think I should buy, ________ blue ones here or ________ red ones over there?

4 ________ toffees I'm eating are great!

5 – Look here, boys and girls. I found _______ test in the playground. Whose is it?

– ________ is my test, Miss Jolly. I lost it yesterday.

– No, Tom. ________ isn't your test. ________ is your test over there. But isn't ________ your writing, Sally? I think ________ is your test.

– No, Miss Jolly. ________ is not my test. _______ is my test. It was in my bag.

1 (this) – (that)
2 that – that – That
3 these – those
4 These
5 this – That – This – That – this – this – That – This

Das Datum von heute __________

61 Pronomen gemischt

Wer hat hier einen Streich gespielt? Jemand hat alle Pronomen aus dem Brief entfernt. Schreibe sie nochmals in den Brief, sonst ist der Sinn nicht klar.
Hier sind die fehlenden Pronomen:

I *(6 x)* – it *(1 x)* – me *(4 x)* – my *(4 x)* – our *(1 x)* – them *(1 x)* – they *(2 x)* – you *(4 x)* – your *(3 x)* – we *(3 x)*

Dear Sue,

How are ________ [1]? You ________ haven't had a letter from ________ [2] for a long time so ________ [3] thought ________ [4] would write ________ [5] a letter.

________ [6] parents have gone to France on holiday so ________ [7] am alone at home. ________ [8] wrote a postcard to ________ [9] and ________ [10] are having great weather. Where are ________ [11] parents going on holiday this year? Are you going with ________ [12]? ________ [13] couldn't go with ________ [14] parents because of ________ [15] dog.

________ [16] friends and I are going to London for a week and ________ [17] think ________ [18] will all have a great time. Why don't ________ [19] come to London, too? _____ [20] can all stay at the same place. Isn't that a great idea? Ask ________ [21] parents and let ________ [22] know soon. ________ [23] are in London for the third week of August.

________ [24] will be real fun!

All ________ [25] love, and please say HELLO to ________ [26] family from ________ [27].

Alison

G 5/6

1 you
2 me
3 I
4 I
5 you
6 My

7 I
8 They
9 me
10 they
11 your
12 them

13 I
14 my
15 our
16 My
17 I
18 we

19 you
20 We
21 your
22 me
23 We
24 It

25 my
26 your
27 me

Das Datum von heute ___________

62 Gesteigerte Adjektive

Vervollständige die Tabelle mit den Steigerungsformen der angegebenen Adjektive.

Adjektiv	Komparativ	Superlativ
1 bad		
2 beautiful	more beautiful	most beautiful
3 careful		
4 cheap	cheaper	cheapest
5 easy		
6 good		
7 interesting		
8 large		
9 lovely		
10 many		

1 worse, worst
2 (more beautiful), (most beautiful)
3 more careful, most careful
4 (cheaper), (cheapest)
5 easier, easiest
6 better, best
7 more interesting, most interesting
8 larger, largest
9 lovelier, loveliest
10 more, most

G 5/6

Das Datum von heute ____________

63 Komparativ oder Superlativ?

Setze die Komparativ- oder Superlativform der Adjektive in die Sätze ein.

1 – Sam and Eric are twins, but Sam is the ______________ (big) of the two.

– Yes, but Eric is the ______________ (clever).

2 – Who is the ______________ (kind) teacher here?

– Miss Jolly. She is the ______________ (nice) teacher I know.

3 – I got a ______________ (good) mark in maths today.

– So what? That was the ______________ (easy) test we've ever had. Last week's test was ______________ (difficult).

4 – I don't like Dirk. He's the ______________ (nasty) boy I know. And the ______________ (silly), too.

– Oh, come on. I know lots of ______________ (bad) boys.

5 – Can I have ______________ (many) chips, please?

– No. You've had the ______________ (many) already.

6 – What's ______________ (interesting), TV or reading?

– Well, TV can be OK, but a good book is ________________________________ (exciting), I think.

G 5/6

1 bigger – cleverer
2 kindest – nicest
3 better – easiest – more difficult
4 nastiest – silliest – worse
5 more – most
6 more interesting – more exciting

Das Datum von heute ___________

64 Adjektive vergleichen

Übersetze die unterstrichenen Teile der Sätze ins Englische.

1 Ein BMW ist nicht so teuer wie ein Porsche.

Porsche baut die teuersten Autos in Deutschland.

2 Basketball ist so spannend wie Handball, aber ist nicht so hart.

3 Die Mädchen waren besser und intelligenter als die Jungen.

Sie waren im Turnier die Besten und haben den schönsten Pokal *(cup)* gewonnen.

4 Unser Klassenlehrer ist nicht sehr freundlich.

Unser alter Lehrer war viel netter und interessanter.

Jetzt haben wir einen der strengsten Lehrer der Schule.

1 not as expensive as – the most expensive
2 as exciting as – not as hard
3 better and more intelligent than – the best – the most beautiful cup
4 is not very friendly – much nicer and more interesting – one of the strictest teachers

Das Datum von heute ____________

65 Farben

Jetzt testen wir dein Allgemeinwissen. Alle Antworten sind Farben.

1 What are the colours of the British flag?

____

2 What colour is a kiwi fruit? ______________________________

3 What colour are traffic lights when you mustn't go? ______________________________

____

4 What are the five primary colours *(Grundfarben)?*

____

5 What two colours make green? ______________________________

6 What colour is the Queen's blood? ______________________________

7 What colour does black and white make? ______________________________

8 What colour is a crocodile? ______________________________

9 What are the colours of the German flag?

____

10 What colour is a 100 €-note? ______________________________

11 And a 50 €-note? ______________________________

Weitere Fragen. Dieses Mal stecken die Farben in den Fragen.

12 What is yellow and dangerous?

____

13 What is yellow and jumps from tree to tree?

____

14 What is green and goes up and down?

____

1 Red, white and blue
2 brown
3 red, yellow
4 red, blue, yellow, black, white
5 yellow and blue
6 red (blue!)
7 grey
8 dark green
9 black, red and gold
10 green
11 brown
12 a Banana with a gun
13 Marzipan, Tarzan's brother
14 an apple in a lift *(Aufzug)*

G 5/6

Das Datum von heute ___________

66 Adverbien – regelmäßige und unregelmäßige

Bilde Adverbien von den Adjektiven:

1 slow ______________________

2 angry ______________________

3 easy ______________________

4 beautiful ______________________

5 quiet ______________________

6 quick ______________________

7 lucky ______________________

8 thirsty ______________________

9 awful ______________________

10 dirty ______________________

1 slowly
2 angrily
3 easily
4 beautifully
5 quietly
6 quickly
7 luckily
8 thirstily
9 awfully
10 dirtily

Das Datum von heute ____________

67 Passende Adverbien im Text

Suche dir ein passendes Adjektiv, bilde sein Adverb und setze es dann ein.

bad – beautiful – careful – good – easy – quiet – thirsty – ~~happy~~ – quick

1 The boys went on holiday happily . No more school!

2 Freddy drank the lemonade ________________ . He was hot.

3 Sally did her homework ________________ . She is a good pupil,

4 Bob ran home ________________ . It only took him seven minutes.

5 Elvira listened to her records ________________ . Mrs Nunn was asleep.

6 Sally plays the piano ________________ .

She will ________________ win the competition *(Wettbewerb)*.

7 Oh dear, Bob sang that song ________________ .

I don't think he can sing very ________________ .

G 5/6

2 thirstily
3 carefully
4 quickly
5 quietly
6 beautifully – easily
7 badly – well

Das Datum von heute ___________

68 Sätze mit Adverbien

Schreibe Sätze mit Adverbien.

1 Sally is a careful learner. (learn)

Sally learns carefully.

2 Bob is a good football player. (play football)

Bob plays well football

3 Tom is a fast runner. (run)

Tom runns fast

4 Freddy is a bad swimmer. (swim)

Freddy swimms badly

5 Mr Cobb is a hard worker. (work)

Mr Cobb works hard

6 Freddy is a thirsty drinker. (drink)

Freddy drinks thirstily

2 plays football well.
3 runs fast.
4 swims badly.
5 works hard.
6 drinks thirstily.

G 5/6

Das Datum von heute ____________

69 Adverb oder Adjektiv?

Entscheide, ob du ein Adjektiv oder ein Adverb benötigst.

1 (sad) 'Why are you so ___sad___, Sally?'
'I've lost Spooky', said Sally ___sadly___.

2 (kind) Because Tom was a ___kind___ boy, he said ___kindly___: 'Well, I'll help you to find him.'

3 (quiet) 'Bob, be ___quiet___, please. Play your records ___quietly___ or go outside.'

4 (hungry) 'Here comes Freddy. He looks ___hungrily___,' said Mrs Cobb.
'Hello, Mrs Cobb. That cake smells good,' said Freddy ___hungry___.

5 (quiet) Sally spoke very ___quietly___ in lessons so Miss Jolly couldn't hear her. 'Don't talk so ___quiet___,' she said. 'I can't understand you.'

6 (good) Sally works ___well___ at school.
She is a ___good___ pupil.

1 sad – sadly
2 kind – kindly
3 quiet – quietly
4 hungry – hungrily
5 quietly – quietly
6 well – good

70 Die Steigerung der Adverbien

Schreibe den Komparativ und den Superlativ zu den Adverbien auf.

Adjektiv	Komparativ	Superlativ
1 quickly	more quickly	
2 fast		
3 well		
4 beautifully		
5 early		
6 hard		
7 nastily		
8 badly		
9 terribly		
10 easily		

1 (more quickly) – most quickly
2 faster – fastest
3 better – best
4 more beautifully – most beautifully
5 earlier – earliest
6 harder – hardest
7 more nastily – most nastily
8 worse – worst
9 more terribly – most terribly
10 more easily – most easily

Das Datum von heute __________

71 Gesteigerte Adverbien im Satz

Setze die richtige Form des gesteigerten Adverbs ein.

1 I work more happily (happily) when the sun is shining than when it is raining.

2 Miss Jolly drives ____________________ (carefully) than Mr Carter.

3 You always work ____________________ (well) than most but today you did the ____________________ (well).

4 Tom can run ____________________ (fast) than Freddy.

5 Can't you play your music ____________________ (quiet) than you always do?

6 The school team played ____________________ (badly) than they did last week.

7 Elvira worked ____________________ (hard) than the other pupils and got the best mark.

8 Tom jumped ____________________ (high) than Bob but Elvira jumped 2 cm ____________________ (high). She jumped the ____________________ (high) in the form, in fact.

G 5/6

2 more carefully
3 better – best
4 faster
5 more quietly (quieter)
6 worse
7 harder
8 higher – higher – highest

Das Datum von heute __________

72 Puzzle mit Adverbien

Zuerst vervollständige die Sätze unten, um herauszufinden, welche Adverbien du in das Puzzle eintragen sollst. Wenn du sie richtig eingesetzt hast, kannst du das Suchwort in den markierten Feldern von oben nach unten lesen.

1 Tom did very b__________ in the maths test. He got 1 out of 10.

2 Bob, I can't even read this. Why can't you write n__________?

3 I'm tired. I've worked really h__________ today.

4 Play q__________. Mum's asleep.

5 Spooky can run much f__________ than Coco.

6 Elvira was the best. She won the competition e__________.

7 In the supermarket: All fruit f__________ picked *(frisch)*.

8 We must walk more q__________. We're late.

9 Sally did very w__________. She got 9 out of 10.

10 Can't you hurry up? You're working so s__________ that we'll never finish.

11 Spooky always barks l__________ when the postman comes.

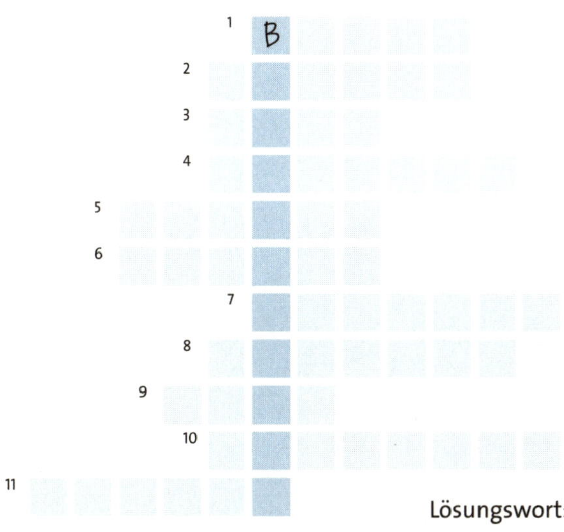

Lösungswort: ____________________

1 (b)adly
2 (n)eatly
3 (h)ard
4 (q)uietly
5 (f)aster
6 (e)asily
7 (f)reshly
8 (q)uickly
9 (w)ell
10 (s)lowly
11 (l)oudly

Lösungswort: beautifully

Das Datum von heute ___________

73 Wortstellung in Aussagesätzen

In Aussagesätzen lautet die Grundstellung immer **Subjekt – Verb – Objekt** (**S**traßen**v**erkehrs**o**rdnung/**SVO**). Der Schreibcomputer hat hier wieder verrückt gespielt! Er hat oft die Satzteile durcheinandergebracht. Kannst du seine Fehler finden und die Satzteile mit Ziffern richtig ordnen?

1 (3) baking cakes (2) likes (1) Mrs Nunn

2 ( ) a lot of toffees ( ) eats ( ) Freddy

3 ( ) likes ( ) Spooky ( ) playing with balls

4 ( ) Mr Pratt ( ) his new car ( ) is washing

5 ( ) is reading ( ) Ms Jolly ( ) a book

6 ( ) Mr and Mrs Cobb ( ) gardening ( ) enjoy

G
5/6

2 3-2-1
3 2-1-3
4 1-3-2
5 2-1-3
6 1-3-2

Das Datum von heute ___________

74 Orts- und Zeitangaben im Satz

Benutze Ziffern, um die Orts-/Zeitangaben am Ende der Sätze in die richtige Reihenfolge zu setzen.

1 The Cobb children go ___ (2) in Kingston ___ (1) to school ___

2 We are all going ___ ( ) in London ___ ( ) on Saturday ___ ( ) to the cinema ___

3 Mr Nunn goes ___ ( ) at 7 o'clock ___ ( ) every day ___ ( ) to work ___

4 The film starts ___ ( ) at 8.30 ___ ( ) at the youth club ___ ( ) on Friday ___

5 We will see you ___ ( ) at Elvira's party ___ ( ) tonight ___

6 Freddy is going ___ ( ) in Greece ___ ( ) this summer ___ ( ) to Athens ___

7 Miss Jolly is moving ___ ( ) at the weekend ___ ( ) in Penny Street ___ ( ) to her new flat ___

2 2-3-1
3 2-3-1
4 2-1-3
5 1-2
6 2-3-1
7 3-2-1

75 Adverbien der Häufigkeit

In der Regel stellen wir Häufigkeitsadverbien wie *often, usually* und *sometimes* unmittelbar vor das Vollverb. Setze das Häufigkeitsadverb in Klammern mit einem Pfeil ein.

1 (sometimes) Tom ○ forgets ○ his maths homework ○ .

2 (often) Sally and Elvira ○ go ○ dancing ○ on Fridays ○ .

3 (every week) Bob and Tom ○ meet ○ at the youth club ○ in Davis Street ○ .

4 (sometimes) Mr Nunn ○ helps ○ Mrs Nunn ○ with the cooking ○ on Sundays ○ .

5 (always) Mrs Pratt ○ drives ○ very carefully ○ .

6 (never) Spooky ○ is ○ a naughty little dog ○ .

G
5/6

2 *hinter* Elvira
3 *ganz am Satzende*
4 *hinter* Mr Nunn
5 *hinter* Mr Pratt
6 *hinter* is

Das Datum von heute ___________

76 Zahlen (Kardinalzahlen)

Beantworte diese Fragen. Schreibe die Zahlen bitte voll aus.

1 How many days are there in a year?

three hundred and sixty-five

2 How much is 35 and 46?

____

3 How many days are there in July?

____

4 How many states are there in the USA?

____

5 How many months are there in a year?

____

6 How many legs does a spider *(Spinne)* have?

____

7 How many colours are there in a rainbow *(Regenbogen)?*

____

8 How much is 27 and 23?

____

9 How many kilometres is it from Hamburg to Munich *(München)?*

____

2 eighty-one
3 thirty-one
4 fifty
5 twelve
6 eight
7 seven
8 fifty
9 seven hundred and eighty-two!

G
5/6

Das Datum von heute ____________

77 Zahlen (Ordinalzahlen)

Ordinalzahlen beantworten die Frage nach dem/der ... Wievielten? Beantworte die Fragen, dann nimm den gewünschten Buchstaben heraus und schreibe ihn unten auf.
Die Buchstaben ergeben aneinandergereiht einen Satz.

1 The third letter of the tenth month of the year. T

2 The second letter of the fourth day of the week. ______

3 The fourth letter of the fourth month of the year. ______

4 The sixth letter of the third day of the week. ______

5 The third letter of the fifth day of the week. ______

6 The fifth letter of the eighth month of the year. ______

7 The seventh letter of the twelfth month of the year. ______

8 The seventh letter of the sixth day of the week. ______

9 The sixth letter of the third day of the week. ______

10 The eighth letter of the second month of the year. ______

Dein Satz: T ____________________________

G 5/6

1 (T)
2 H
3 I
4 S
5 I
6 S
7 E
8 A
9 S
10 Y
Dein Satz: This is easy.

Das Datum von heute ____________

78 Der wievielte Buchstabe?

Der wievielte Buchstabe im Alphabet ist es? Schreibe es auf.

1 E is fifth .

2 N is ____________ .

3 G is ____________ .

4 L is ____________ .

5 I is ____________ .

6 S is ____________ .

7 C is ____________ .

8 H is ____________ .

9 W is ____________ .

10 O is ____________ .

11 R is ____________ .

12 T is ____________ .

2 fourteenth
3 seventh
4 twelfth
5 ninth
6 nineteenth
7 third
8 eighth
9 twenty-third
10 fifteenth
11 eighteenth
12 twentieth

Das Datum von heute ____________

79 Quiz mit Zahlen

Die Fragen haben alle irgendetwas mit Großbritannien zu tun. Die Antworten dazu sind alle Zahlen.
Sicherlich kannst du mehrere Fragen sofort richtig beantworten. Andere Fragen sind schwieriger, aber gib trotzdem nicht auf. Deine Eltern oder Lehrer werden dir sicherlich helfen!

The Queen

1 In what year was Queen Elizabeth born? ○ 1920 ○ 1924 ○ 1926

2 How many children has the Queen got? ____________

3 How many British queens are called Elizabeth? ____________

London

4 How many people live in London? ○ 6 million ○ 7 million ○ 8 million

5 How many clock faces *(Zifferblatt)* has Big Ben got? ____________

6 How many different lines has the London underground got?

○ 9 ○ 10 ○ 11

The Island of Britain

7 About how long is the coast of Britain? ____________

8 About how many islands are there round Britain's coast?

○ 500 ○ 250 ○ 400

9 How long is Britain from north to south?

○ 800 km ○ 1000 km ○ 1200 km

10 How many different countries are there in Britain? ____________

11 About how long is the River Thames? ○ 250 km ○ 300 km ○ 350 km

12 About how high is Ben Nevis, Britain's highest mountain?

○ 1100 m ○ 1300 m ○ 1500 m

G
5/6

1 1926
2 4
3 2
4 7 million
5 none (Big Ben ist keine Uhr. Es ist eine Glocke)
6 11
7 2500 km
8 500
9 1200 km
10 4 (England, Northern Ireland, Scotland, Wales)
11 350 km
12 1300 m

Das Datum von heute ____________

80 Mengenangaben

	⊞	⊟	?
zählbar	a lot of lots of	(not) many	many
nicht zählbar	a lot of lots of	(not) much	much

1 Unterstreiche die folgenden Wörter **nur,** wenn sie **nicht zählbar** sind.

apple – bag – book – <u>bread</u> – butter – chalk – child – coffee – exercise *(Bewegung)* – exercise *(Übung)* – girl – homework – horse – love – meat – milk – money – orange – paper – penny – sugar – time *(Zeit)* – tea – water – wine

2 Setze *much, many* oder *a lot of* in die Sätze ein.

1 Freddy spends ____________________ money on toffees.

2 Do you know ____________________ people in Germany?

3 We don't have ____________________ time. Hurry up!

4 Bob hasn't got ____________________ money with him, but he's got quite ____________________ money in his savings account *(Sparkonto)*.

5 How ____________________ bottles of lemonade did Sally buy?

6 __________________ boys play football but not __________________ girls play it.

1 (bread) – butter – chalk – coffee – exercise (Bewegung) – homework – love – meat – milk – money – paper – sugar – time – tea – water – wine

2 1 a lot of
2 many
3 much
4 much – a lot of
5 many
6 A lot of – many

G 5/6

81 Dialog mit Mengenangaben

Setze *some, any, much, many* oder *a lot of* in den Dialog ein.

Mrs C I'm going to Bunn's. Do you need __________ food ?

Mrs P Yes, can you buy me __________ sugar, please?

Mrs C Of course. How __________ sugar do you want?

Mrs P Just 1 kilo, please. Oh, and we haven't got __________ eggs.
Could you bring me __________ eggs, too, please?

Mrs C OK. How __________ do you want?

Mrs P A dozen. Oh, and I need __________ cheese. Bring __________ cheese, please, because I want to make cheese salads tonight.

Mrs C Yes, all right. I'll bring __________ cheese, too, then.
What about butter? Do you need __________ butter?

Mrs P Yes, of course. Thank you. I haven't got __________ butter, either.

Mrs C What a surprise! How __________ should I get?

Mrs P Just half a pound, please. Oh, and __________ bananas, I …

Mrs C Look, this is quite __________ of shopping.
Why don't you come to Bunn's with me?

Mrs P I haven't got __________ time, dear.
I have such __________ things to do, and
I haven't got __________ help at all.

any – some – much – any – some – many – some – a lot of – a lot of/some – some – any – any – much –
some – a lot of – any – a lot of – any

Das Datum von heute ___________

82 Somebody, something, somewhere und anybody, anything, anywhere

Lies die Sätze durch und trage eine sinnvolle Zusammensetzung von *some/any* ein.

1 I am very hungry. Can I have something to eat, please?

2 Tom can't see Spooky ______________ but he knows he's in the garden ______________ because he can hear him.

3 Is there ______________ there? I heard ______________ cough *(husten)*.

4 – I can't find my pen ______________. Can I have yours?

– No, you can't. I'm never going to give you ______________ again, because you never give things back.

2 anywhere – somewhere
3 anyone/anybody – someone/somebody
4 anywhere – anything

G 5/6

Das Datum von heute __________

83 *Some*, *any* und ihre Zusammensetzungen

Setze *some, any* oder eine ihrer Zusammensetzungen in die Sätze ein.

1 I haven't got ____________ lemonade but I can give you ____________ cold milk.

2 – Miss Jolly can't find her purse ____________ but it must be ____________ in the classroom.

– Or do you think that ____________ took it?

3 Freddy's so lazy. He never does ____________ work.

4 – Have you got ____________ money?

– Well, I've got ____________ at home.

5 – Can ____________ here speak German?

6 Sally can give you ____________ books to read. Bob hasn't got ____________ books at all.

7 There's ____________ wrong with our car.

Can you do ____________ about it?

G
5/6

1 any – some
2 anywhere – somewhere – somebody/someone
3 any
4 any – some
5 anyone/anybody
6 some – any
7 something – anything

Das Datum von heute __________

84 Präpositionen des Ortes

above	*über*	near	*nah*
at	*an*	next to	*neben*
behind	*hinter*	on	*auf*
between	*zwischen*	outside	*draußen*
in front of	*vor*	round	*rund (um)*
inside	*in*	under	*unter*

Beschreibe, wo die Kinder in Miss Jollys Klasse sitzen.
Hier sind ihre Schreibtische mit Namenskarten.

1 Sally sits next to Elvira.

2 Freddy sits __________ Tom and Mike.

3 Bob sits __________ Susan.

4 Mike sits __________ Freddy.

5 Mike sits __________ John and Susan.

6 Dirk sits __________ John.

7 Tom sits __________ Elvira.

8 Jane sits __________ Sally.

9 Bob sits __________ Freddy and Jane.

10 Dirk sits __________ Freddy.

2 between
3 in front of
4 behind
5 between
6 in front of
7 next to
8 behind
9 between
10 next to

G 5/6

Das Datum von heute ________

85 Präpositionen der Zeit

at	4 o'clock/6.30/...	*Uhrzeit*
at	night	*nachts*
at	the weekend	*am Wochenende*
at	Christmas/Easter/...	*religiöse Feste*
on	Monday/Tuesday/...	*Wochentage*
on	March 14th/September 2nd/...	*Daten*
in	the morning/afternoon/evening	*Tageszeit*
in	May/June/...	*Monate*
in	spring/summer/...	*Jahreszeit*
in	1066/1974/...	*Jahreszahl*

Trage *in*, *at* oder *on* ein.

1 Freddy often goes to bed late _____ night and gets up early _____ the morning.

2 He eats breakfast _____ a few minutes during the week but _____ the weekend he has lots of time.

3 He was born _____ 7th July 1974.

4 He always goes to Spain _____ the summer but he stays at home _____ Christmas and _____ Easter.

5 It often snows _____ winter.

6 So Freddy often goes skiing _____ the weekend _____ January.

7 He sometimes goes swimming with his friends _____ Saturdays _____ the summer.

G 5/6

1 at – in
2 in – at
3 on
4 in – at – at
5 in
6 at – in
7 on – in

Das Datum von heute ____________

86 Präpositionen gemischt

Übersetze die unterstrichenen Präpositionen ins Englische.

1 Ich komme um 5 Uhr. ____________

2 In England ist Weihnachten am 25. Dezember. ____________

3 Ich sah Julia letztes Jahr im Juli. ____________

4 Der Test ist am Freitag um 9 Uhr. ____________

5 Ein Baum steht vor dem Haus. ____________

6 Die Familie sitzt am Tisch. ____________

7 Mr Carter kam uns entgegen. ____________

8 Du sollst am besten um London fahren. ____________

9 Bob lief die Straße runter. ____________

10 Der Ball ging über den Zaun und durch das Fenster. ____________

11 Die Cobbs wohnen neben den Pratts. ____________

12 Sally wurde 1975 in Kingston geboren. ____________

1 at
2 on
3 in
4 on – at
5 in front of
6 at
7 towards
8 round
9 down
10 over – through
11 next to
12 in (1975) – in

G 5/6

Das Datum von heute __________

87 Simple past: Fragen mit und ohne Fragewort

1 Lies dir Shanes Brief durch.

Dear Tim, London, 25th August

Thank you for your letter. Now I can answer all your questions. I went <u>to Spain</u> on holiday this summer. No, I didn't go alone. I went with my parents. We stayed there <u>for two weeks</u>. The weather was <u>sunny and warm</u>. Yes, I went swimming every day. No, the water wasn't very cold. Yes, I met a lot of girls. I <u>played volleyball</u> with them. No, I didn't see any sharks. That's a silly question. There are no sharks in Spain.

I got back to London <u>on 20th August</u>.

Love, Shane

2 Schreibe du jetzt Tims Brief, auf den Shane hier geantwortet hat.
Du sollst noch neun Fragen formulieren. Nach den unterstrichenen Angaben in Shanes Brief musst mit dem richtigen Fragewort fragen, z. B. *to Spain* → *Where.*

Dear Shane,

Where did you go on holiday this summer?

____

____

____

____

____

____

____

____

Love,

G 5/6

2 Did you go alone? How long did you stay? What was the weather like? Did you go swimming every day? Was the water very cold? Did you meet a lot of girls? What did you play with them? Did you see any sharks? When did you get back to London?

Das Datum von heute __________

88 Simple present und simple past

This is an interview with the famous basketball player Michaela Garden.

Trage die folgenden Formen von *to do* in den Text ein.
Eine Form von *to do* bleibt übrig. Welche ist es? Trage sie hier ein: __________

do – did – do – doesn't – do – didn't – do – doesn't – did – do – does – do – do – does – does – did – don't – doesn't – didn't

Interviewer: "Hello, Mrs Garden. I'd like to ask you some questions. When ________[1] you start playing basketball?" • Michaela: "I started playing basketball fifteen years ago." • I.: "__________[2] you join a basketball club when you were six?" • M.: "No, I __________[3]. I played in the streets." • "I.: How often ________[4] you play basketball now?" • M.: "Normally I play five times a week." I.: "_______[5] you have any brothers or sisters?" • M.: "Yes, I ___________[6]. I have one brother." • I.: "__________[7] he play basketball, too?" • M.: "No, he ___________[8]. He hates it." • I.: "__________[9] your parents like basketball?" • M.: "Yes, they ___________[10]." • I.: "___________[11] your father read a lot about basketball?" • M.: "Yes, he __________[12]. He reads a lot, but he _______[13] watch basketball games on TV." • I.: "___________[14] your father play basketball when he was young?" • M.: "No, he ___________[15]. He wasn't tall enough." • I.: "_______[16] you eat anything special before a basketball game?" • M.: "No, I ___________[17]. I eat whatever I like." • I.: "When ________[18] you go to bed?" • M.: "I go to bed at nine o'clock." • I.: "Thank your for the interview, Mrs Garden."

1 did
2 Did
3 didn't
4 do
5 Do
6 do
7 Does
8 doesn't
9 Do
10 do
11 Does
12 does
13 doesn't
14 Did
15 didn't
16 Do
17 don't
18 do
Doesn't bleibt übrig.

G 5/6

Das Datum von heute __________

89 Will-future

1 Die ganze Familie Floyd denkt über das nächste Jahr nach. Sie haben sehr unterschiedliche Erwartungen, Hoffnungen und auch Befürchtungen. Bilde aus den angegebenen Satzteilen Sätze mit dem *will-future*.

Mr. Floyd: to buy / next year / a new car

I think I will buy a new car next year.

1 Mrs Floyd: I / to do / next year / more sports I think __________

____

2 Tom: daddy / to buy / next year / a new car I hope __________

____

3 Grandpa Floyd: to be / the next year / a cold year. I think __________

____

4 Jane: my own room / I / to get / next year I think __________

____

5 Maxi, Jane's dog: to move / next year / to the country / the family

Maybe the family __________

2 Einige in der Familie haben gute Vorsätze für das nächste Jahr. Bilde Sätze mit dem *will-future*.

1 Jane: for a walk / the dog / more often *(öfter)* / to take / next year

I promise I will __________

2 Mr Floyd: to go shopping / once a week *(einmal in der Woche)* / next year

I promise __________

3 Grandpa Floyd: in the living room / to stop / smoking cigars / next year

I promise __________

G 5/6

1 1 I think I will do more sports next year.
2 I hope daddy will buy a new car next year.
3 I think the next year will be a cold year.
4 I think I will get my own room next year.
5 Maybe the family will move to the country next year.

2 1 I promise I will take the dog for a walk more often next year.
2 I promise I will go shopping once a week next year.
3 I promise I will stop smoking cigars in the living room next year.

90 Going to-future

Tom is with his parents in Wales, at the foot of Snowdon*.
He wants to climb Snowdon tomorrow. He phones his friend Shane
to find out what the weather will be like.

** Mount Snowdon is the highest mountain in Wales and England.*

Ergänze die Lücken mithilfe der angegebenen Textteile aus dem Wetterbericht unten im Kasten in dem Gespräch zwischen Shane und Tom.

Tom: "Hi, Shane. Did you see the weather forecast on TV? I want to know what the weather is going to be like on Mount Snowdon." • Shane: "Hi, Tom. Well, in London it's [1] ______________________ heavy rain." • Tom: "I don't want to know about London. It is going to rain in North Wales, isn't it?" • Shane: "Wait a minute. In Scotland it [2] ______________________." • Tom: "Not Scotland: what about Mount Snowdon?" • Shane: "In the east of England it's [3] ______________________" • Tom: "No, not England. Listen: I am in North Wales!" • Shane: "Oh, oh. In Northern Ireland it [4] ______________________." • Tom: "Shane! What about Mount Snowdon?" • Shane: "Why do you want to know? What are you going to do there?" • Tom: "I [5] ______________________ Mount Snowdon tomorrow. Now tell me what the weather [6] ______________________ like for Mount Snowdon tomorrow." • Shane: "Have you got a good anorak with you?" • Tom: "Yes, is it going to rain?" • Shane: "No, it [7] ______________________. So you can leave your anorak at your hotel!"

London: very overcast with heavy rain = stark bewölkt mit strömendem Regen; *Wales: glorious sunshine* = strahlender Sonnenschein; *Scotland: sunny and a bit cloudy* = sonnig und leicht bewölkt; *Northern Ireland: cloudy, rain with some sunny spells* = bewölkt, Regen mit sonnigen Abschnitten; *the east of England: rainy*

1 going to be very overcast with heavy rain;
2 is going to be sunny and a bit cloudy;
3 going to be rainy ODER going to rain;
4 is going to be cloudy and rainy with some sunny spells ODER is going to rain a little bit;
5 am going to climb;
6 is going to be;
7 isn't going to rain.

G 5/6

Das Datum von heute ____________

91 going to- and will-future

Ergänze die Lücken mit der richtigen Futurform des Verbs in Klammern.

1 I think it ________________[1] (to be) an interesting game tonight.

2 I'm sure Schalke ___________________________[2] (to win).

3 My Dad _____________________________[3] (to watch) the game with me on TV.

4 My sister _______________________________[4] (not to watch) the game with us. She hates football.

5 She _________[5] probably _________[5] (to tell) us again how stupid football is.

6 I hope one day she ___________________________________[6] (to understand) us.

7 Maybe Daddy ____[7] (to tell) her some interesting things about football.

8 It ______________________[8] (to be) hard, but he ______________________[9] (to try).

9 Maybe we ___________________________________[10] (to watch) football with the whole family one day!

10 But tonight Mum and my sister ____________________[11] (to go) to the cinema.

1 will be;
2 will win;
3 is going to watch;
4 is not going to watch;
5 will probably tell;
6 will understand;
7 will tell;
8 will be;
9 is going to try
10 will watch;
11 are going to go.

Das Datum von heute 15.02.09

92 Present perfect negative statements

It's 3 o'clock p. m., a sunny Monday afternoon.
Here's Susan's homework list for this week.

1 do maths homework
2 learn some history
3 finish the picture
4 buy a new exercise book
5 draw a map of Great Britain
6 collect some flowers
7 learn my English vocabulary
8 repair my school bag
9 write a story
10 write a German essay
11 make a survey about the traffic in our town
12 read the end of the book about Robin Hood

On her way home from school Susan met her friend Lorraine.
The two girls went to a cafeteria and had a lemonade.
Now it's 5 o'clock p. m. Look at Susan's homework list.

Schreibe auf, was Susan alles noch nicht getan hat.

1 I haven't done my maths homework yet.
2 I haven't learned some history yet.
3 I haven't finished the picture yet.
4 I haven't bought a new execrise book yet
5 I haven't drawn a map of Great Britan yet.
6 I haven't collected some flowers yet
7 I haven't learned my English vocabulary yet
8 I haven't repaired my school bag yet
9 I haven't written a German essay yet.
10 I haven't made a survey about the tr. in our town yet.
11 I haven't
12

2 I haven't learned any history yet.
3 I haven't finished the picture yet.
4 I haven't bought a new exercise book yet.
5 I haven't drawn a map of Great Britain yet.
6 I haven't collected any flowers yet.
7 I haven't learned my English vocabulary yet.
8 I haven't repaired my school bag yet.
9 I haven't written a story yet.
10 I haven't written a German essay yet.
11 I haven't made a survey about the traffic in our town yet.
12 I haven't read the end of the book about Robin Hood yet.

G 5/6

Das Datum von heute 15.02.09

93 Present perfect questions

Jane möchte gerne einen zweiten Hund zu Hause haben, damit Maxi nicht so alleine ist. Aber der Hundezüchter *(the dog breeder)* verkauft nicht jedem einen Hund. Erst vergewissert er sich, dass der Kunde etwas von Tieren versteht.

Ergänze die Fragen, indem du die Verben im *present perfect* schreibst. Im *present perfect* muss nur *have / has* vor das Subjekt an den Anfang des Satzes gestellt werden, um eine Frage zu bilden:
Has she gone home already? Ist sie schon nach Hause gegangen?

1 Dog breeder: "Have you ever had a pet?" (to have)
• Jane: "Yes, we have always had several dogs at home."

2 Dog breeder: "Have you always kept your dogs in the house?" (to keep) • Jane: "Yes, we have."

3 Dog breeder: "Have you ever sold one of your dogs?" (to sell)
• Jane: "No, of course not."

4 Dog breeder: "Have you always given your dog proper food?" (to give)
• Jane: "Yes, we have always given our dogs good dog-food."

5 Dog breeder: "Why have you decided to buy another dog?" (to decide) • Jane: "Because our dog Maxi needs a friend to play with."

6 Dog breeder: "Why have you come to me?" (to come)
• Jane: "Because I have heard that you're a good breeder but you ask a lot of questions, don't you?"

G 5/6

1 Have you ever had a pet?
2 Have you always kept your dogs in the house?
3 Have you ever sold one of your dogs?
4 Have you always given your dog proper food?
5 Why have you decided to buy another dog?
6 Why have you come to me?

Das Datum von heute 11.05.08

94 Present perfect – simple past

Entscheide, ob in den folgenden Sätzen das Verb im *present perfect* oder *simple past* geschrieben werden muss.

Mrs Floyd and her husband are in the bank. They are talking to the bank manager. • Bank manager: "Good morning. Can I help you?" • Mrs Floyd: "Yes, we booked [1] (to book) a holiday in Canada three months ago and picked up [2] (pick up) the tickets from the travel agent four weeks later. But we haven't got [3] (to have not got) any Canadian money yet." Bank manager: "Have [4] you decide [4] (to decide) how much you need?" • Mrs Floyd: "We talked [5] (to talk) about that yesterday and we need 5.000 Canadian dollars." • Bank manager: "Did [6] you phone [6] (to phone) us yesterday?" • Mr Floyd: "Yes, we called [7] (to call) in the afternoon." Bank manager: "The money hasn't come [8] (not to come) from the main bank yet." • Mrs Floyd: "That's not good." • Bank manager: "Wait a minute. I checked [9] (to check) an hour ago but perhaps it has come [10] (to come) since then." • Bank manager: "A man has [11] just brought [11] (to bring) the money from the main bank. It is here." • Mr Floyd: "We haven't asked [12] (not to ask) yet how much a Canadian dollar is." • Bank manager: "I checked [13] (to check) yesterday and 5.000 dollars were [14] (to be) 750 pounds. But I haven't looked [15] (not to look) today yet. But I think it's the same." Mr Floyd: "That's OK. Thank you."

1 booked
2 picked up
3 haven't got
4 Have you decided
5 talked
6 Did you phone
7 called
8 hasn't come
9 checked
10 has come
11 has just brought
12 haven't asked
13 checked
14 were
15 haven't looked

G 5/6

95 Mixed tenses I

It's Lorraine's birthday next week.

Lorraine macht sich Gedanken über ihren Geburtstag.
Ergänze in dem folgenden Text die Verben in Klammern in der richtigen Zeit: *simple present, will-future, going to-future, simple past* oder *present perfect*.

What _______[1] I _________[1] (to get) for my 12th birthday next week?

Last year I ___________[2] (to need) a pair of boots, but Mum _________________[3] (to buy) me a new pair of shoes. I _________________[4] (to need) some new T-shirts every year. Mum always ______________[5] (to buy) me a new sweatshirt. Perhaps I _______________________[6] (to get) a new pair of jeans next week. I hope Mum _________________________[7] (to buy) a new skirt for me, too. I'm sure I ________ ______________[8] (to get) some money from my Grandma for my birthday.
I ______________________[9] (to buy) a new pair of basketball trainers then.

1 will I get
2 needed
3 bought
4 need
5 buys
6 will get
7 will buy
8 will get
9 will buy

96 Mixed tenses II

Lorraine wants to buy a new pair of basketball trainers in a sports shop.

Ergänze in dem folgenden Text die Verben in Klammern in der richtigen Zeit: *simple present, will-future, going to-future, simple past* oder *present perfect*.

Shop assistant: "Good afternoon. Can I ________________ (to help) you?" • Lorraine: "I ___________[1] (to need) a new pair of trainers. But I __________________________[2] (not to decide) yet." • Shop assistant: "What size _________[3] you ____________[4] (to take)?" • Lorraine: "Normally I __________________[5] (to take) size 5." • Shop assistant: "_______[6] you ever __________[6] (to have) a pair of Pike trainers?" • Lorraine: "No, I _______________________[7] (not to have)." • Shop assistant: "Last week we __________[8] (to get) the new collection of trainers. They _______[9] (to be) very comfortable. I think I ____________________[10] (to go) and get you a pair of Pike trainers in size 5. Here you are." • Lorraine: "I _______________________[11] (not to like) the colour. I _________[12] (to buy) a nice pair of trainers here last year." • Shop assistant: "Let me see. Yes, the Lions trainers. But I ________[13] (to be) sorry. We _____________ _____________[14] (not to have got) them any more.

We __________[15] (to sell) the last pair of Lions trainers last week. Perhaps we ____________________[16] (to get) some new ones next week." • Lorraine: "OK, perhaps I _____________________[17] (to come) back next week."

1 help
2 need
3 haven't decided
4 do you take
5 take
6 Have you ever had
7 haven't
8 got
9 are
10 will go
11 don't like
12 bought
13 am
14 haven't got
15 sold
16 will get
17 will come

Das Datum von heute __________

97 Satzstellung I

Du kannst dich bestimmt noch erinnern: Im Englischen ist die Satzstellung anders als im Deutschen.

Subjekt – Verb – Objekt – Ortsangaben – Zeitangaben

Für besondere Betonungen können die Satzteile auch manchmal an eine andere Position im Satz wandern. Schreibe die angegebenen Satzteile in der richtigen Satzstellung auf. Denke an die Großschreibung am Satzanfang.

1 to your friends / want to send / do / a letter / you / for Christmas?

Do you want to send a letter to your friends for Christmas?

2 of December / your letters / should send / you / at the beginning

____

3 on the front of / the address / should write / you / the envelope

____

4 the stamp / don't forget / in the right corner / to put

____

5 want to send / by airmail? / do / it / you

____

6 an airmail sticker / put / then / on the envelope

____

G 5/6

2 You should send your letters at the beginning of December.
3 You should write the address on the front of the envelope.
4 Don't forget to put the stamp in the right corner.
5 Do you want to send it by airmail?
6 Put an airmail sticker on the envelope then.

Das Datum von heute __________

98 Satzstellung II

Shane will Postkarten verschicken.
Trage die Satzteile unten in der richtigen Satzstellung an der richtigen Stelle des Gesprächs zwischen Shane und dem Postangestellten ein.
Denke an die Großschreibung am Satzanfang.

( ) very / you / Thank / much.

(1) to Germany? / a postcard / How much / is

( ) for postcards / need / I / 10 stamps / to Germany. •
And / need / for a postcard / I / one stamp / to the USA.

( ) please? / Can / put / on / the airmail sticker / you / for me

( ) to send / I'd like / it / by airmail. / Yes, •
any nice stamps? / Have / got / you

Shane: 1. "How much is ______________________________?"

Post office clerk: "It's 40 p."

Shane: 2. "______________________________

______________________________."

Post office clerk: "Here are ten stamps for the postcards to Germany. Do you want to send the postcard to the USA by airmail?"

Shane: 3. "______________________________.

______________________________?"

Post office clerk: "Yes, I have. You need an airmail sticker, too."

Shane: 4. "______________________________?"

Post office clerk: Yes, of course.

Shane: 5. "______________________________"

1 How much is a postcard to Germany?
2 I need ten stamps for postcards to Germany. And I need one stamp for a postcard to the USA.
3 Yes, I'd like to send it by airmail. Have you got any nice stamps?
4 Can you put on the airmail sticker for me, please?
5 Thank you very much.

Das Datum von heute ____________

99 Present perfect – Aussagen, Fragen, Negativsätze

Bilde Aussagesätze (✔), Negativsätze (✘) oder Fragen (?) im *present perfect* mit den angegebenen Satzteilen.

a Peter / just / do / his homework (✔)
b The boys / go / shopping / yet (?)
c The girls / win / a hockey game / this year (✘)
d your teacher / give back / the English test (?)
e My friend and I / be / in town (✔)
f John / buy / a new exercise book / yet (✘)

a) Peter has just done his homework.
b) Have the boys gone shopping yet?
c) The girls haven't won a hockey game this year.
d) Has your teacher given back the English test?
e) My friend and I have been in town.
f) John hasn't bought a new exercise book yet.

Das Datum von heute __________

100 Zeitformen

1 Schreibe das Verb in die richtige Zeit ein, im *present perfect* oder *simple past*.

On my way home yesterday I ________________ [1] (to see) a big black car. "I ______________ [2] (not to see) that car in our street before," I ____________ [3] (to think). I ______________ [4] (to ask) my father but he ______________ [5] (not to know) the car. So we _____________ [6] (to call) the police. They _____________ [7] (to come) at once. "How often __________ [8] you _________ [8] (to see) that car?" ____________ [9] (to ask) a policeman. "Two times," I ________________ [10] (to say). "Well, somebody ________________ [11] (to steal) this car last week. Mr Thomson _______________ [12] (to report) it a couple of days ago."

2 Streiche die falsche Zeitform durch.

a I think it is going to rain / will rain.
b She bought / has bought a new dress yesterday.
c I haven't done / didn't do my homework yet.
d When my father was a boy he has played / played hockey at school.

1
1 saw;
2 haven't seen;
3 thought;
4 asked;
5 didn't know;
6 called;
7 came;
8 have you seen;
9 asked;
10 said;
11 stole;
12 reported.

2 Die richtigen Zeitformen sind: a) will rain; b) bought; c) haven't done; d) played.

Das Datum von heute __________

101 Halloween (Zeiten)

Es ist Halloween. Shirley Lock ist in New York und hat vom FBI den Auftrag bekommen, sich zu verkleiden wie alle anderen „trick or treaters“ und auf den Straßen nach dem Rechten zu sehen. Aber Shirley kann natürlich auch ihren Spaß haben. Shirley verkleidet sich als Gespenst. Hier sind die Anweisungen, die sie bekommen hat. Ergänze den Text.

whole – twice – as soon as – When – immediately – by sunrise – during – at midnight – after – no longer – day

It's October 31st, and it's Halloween the ______[1] day, so be sure you get up early, at least _____[2]. The real fun doesn't start until ______[3] dark, but _____[4] the day you can practice once or _______[5] saying "Boo!" and scaring people. This has to look authentic! Make sure your jack-o-lantern is finished early, because ______[6] the sun goes down you should light the candle in it. ______[7] it gets dark, put on your ghost costume and go out on the streets.

If your neighbours don't give you a "treat", play a "trick" on them _____[8]. That's the whole point of "trick or treating". Finally, the best place to be ________[9], when the clock strikes twelve, is in a cemetery. You never know ghosts and goblins and witches you might run into there. Have fun!

But be careful! This could be a lucky _____[10] for bad guys. But only up to 12.00, afterwards it's the 31st of October. On the 1st of November it's All Saint's Day *(Allerheiligen)*. It's _________[11] the time for a ghost like you!

V 7/8

1 whole
2 by sunrise
3 after
4 during
5 twice
6 as soon as
7 When
8 immediately
9 at midnight
10 night
11 no longer

Das Datum von heute ____________

102 Once upon a time
(Zeiten und Zahlen)

1 Setze die Begriffe zusammen. Übersetze sie dann und bilde Sätze.

Middle	century
old-	fashioned
15th	Ages
once upon	since
up-to-	date
ever	a time

____

____

____

____

____

____

____

____

____

____

____

____

2 Mache die folgenden Aufgaben, so schnell du kannst.

1 Count to 15 and write all of the numbers here: ______________________________

____

____

2 Put a circle around the odd numbers.
3 Put a box around the even numbers.
4 Write the word for 0.
5 Circle every fifth letter in this sentence.

1 Middle Ages: Mittelalter
once upon a time: es war einmal
up-to-date: auf dem neuesten Stand
15th century: 15. Jahrhundert
old-fashioned: altmodisch
ever since: seitdem, seit

Sample sentences:
Some people wear old-fashioned clothes.
There were knights in the Middle Ages.
His collection of CDs really isn't up-to-date.

2 1 one, two, three, four, five, six, seven, eight, nine, ten, eleven, twelve, thirteen, fourteen, fifteen
2 Odd numbers: one, three, five, seven, nine, eleven, thirteen, fifteen
3 Even numbers: two, four, six, eight, ten, twelve, fourteen
4 Oh, zero
5 l; r; t; t; t; e; c

V 7/8

Das Datum von heute __________

103 A tense story (Zeitformen)

Lies die Geschichte und ergänze die passenden Zeitformen.

Halloween, October 31st, 11.35 pm.

The last of the "trick or treaters" (walk) ______________ [1] tiredly through the neighbourhood on their way home, and the ghost, alias Shirley Lock-Holmes, (draw) _______ [2] a Halloween monster on a window of the last house on Church Street, only wit soap, of course. The neighbours (go) ______________ [3] away the day before and (not leave) ______________ [4] a treat. Very foolish on Halloween! A lot of kids (play) ______________ [5] tricks on them, even before Shirley got there.

Shirley (look) _______________ [6] tiredly at Watson. "We (do) _______________ [7] this for almost six hours, since 6 pm. Now, we (go) ______________ [8] home. And we (not walk) ____________________ [9] through the cemetary. That's for sure!"

Suddenly, she (hear) _________________ [10] screams behind her. "Help! You (steal) _______________ [11] our sweets. Stop! You can't have them! And you're no angel!"

Now she could see it. An angel (try) ________________ [12] to run off with the bags of sweets from a group of young ghosts. Shirley shouted, "Hey! What do you think you (do) _____________ [13] there. You can't do that – not even on Halloween!"

"But an angel never (do) _____________ [14] the wrong thing!" (say) ____________ [15] the thief, and (laugh) ______________ [16] nastily.

"I (hear) _________________ [17] that laugh somewhere before," said Sirley.

"But when and where? Ah, now I (know) _________________ [18]. It's Crazy Cadbury the famous chocolate thief. (not worry) _________________ [19] ghost. I (get) _______________ [20] him for you!" And, of course she (do) ______________ [21].

Shirley always (get) __________ [22] her man. "I (never/catch) _____________ [23] an angel. I guess on Halloween anything can happen!"

V 7/8

1 walked	7 have done	13 are doing	19 Don't worry
2 drew	8 will go	14 does	20 will get
3 had gone	9 won't walk	15 said	21 did
4 had not left	10 heard	16 laughed	22 gets
5 had played	11 have stolen	17 have heard	23 have never caught
6 looked	12 was trying	18 know	

Das Datum von heute ____________

104 Enjoy the break! (Feiertage)

1 Ergänze die Sätze mit den Begriffen im Kasten.

Thanksgiving – A day off – April Fool's Day – ancestors – New Year's Eve – customs and traditions – Parade – Soul

1 A festive march along a street. ______________________

2 You might not hear the truth on this day. ______________________

3 The night before january 1. ______________________

4 Your great-great-grandparents are some of your ______________________ .

5 Any day you don't work. ______________________

6 In your heart, also Afro-American food and music. ______________________

7 In the US, a day for turkey and pumpkin pie. ______________________

8 Every culture has special ______________________ for holidays.

2 Ergänze den Satz.

After you recall the fall *(Herbst)*,

you can ☐☐☐☐☐☐☐☐ November.

1 1 Parade
2 April Fool's Day
3 New Year's Eve
4 ancestors
5 A day off
6 Soul
7 Thanksgiving
8 customs and traditions

2 After you recall the fall, you can *remember* November.

Das Datum von heute ____________

105 Characteristics (Eigenschaften)

Welche der Eigenschaften sollten die folgenden Personen haben? Schreibe sie in den *should be*-Kasten oder in den *shouldn't be*-Kasten.

	should be	shouldn't be
1 the president of your country shy, respectable, bright, stupid, clever, powerful		
2 a teacher patient, impatient, friendly, unfriendly, fair, unfair, intelligent, strict		
3 a boyfriend/girlfriend loyal, true, self-centred, selfish, egoistic, in love with me, pretty		
4 a parent mean, generous, fair, unfair, broke, rich, strict, easy-going, handy		
5 a policewoman brave, courageous, afraid, fair, cruel, ruthless, reliable, careful		
6 a scientist brilliant, practical, reasonable, stupid, foolish, aimless		
7 a shop assistant honest, dishonest, polite, courteous, rude, impolite		
8 a monster cruel, ruthless, awful, peaceful, quiet, noisy, silent, ugly, related to you		

should be
1 respectable, bright, clever, powerful
2 patient, friendly, fair, intelligent
3 loyal, true, in love with me, pretty
4 generous, fair, rich, easy-going, handy
5 brave, courageous, fair, reliable, careful
6 brilliant, reasonable, practical
7 honest, polite, courteous
8 cruel, ruthless, awful, noisy, ugly

shouldn't be
1 shy, stupid
2 impatient, unfriendly, unfair, strict
3 self-centred, selfish, egoistic
4 mean, unfair, broke, strict
5 afraid, cruel, ruthless
6 stupid, foolish, aimless
7 dishonest, rude, impolite
8 peaceful, quiet, silent, related to you

Das Datum von heute ___________

106 Your grandparents (Lebenslauf)

1 Bringe die einzelnen Lebensstationen in eine traditionelle Reihenfolge.

1 ______________________________
2 ______________________________
3 ______________________________
4 ______________________________
5 ______________________________
6 ______________________________
7 ______________________________
8 ______________________________
9 ______________________________
10 ______________________________
11 ______________________________

get divorced
be named
be born
die
get married
take care of your children
start a family
become a student
start school
look after your parents
become a senior citizen

2 Benutze die Verben, um mehrere Sätze über deine Großeltern zu schreiben.

____
____
____
____
____
____
____
____

1
1. be born
2. be named
3. start school
4. become a student
5. get married
6. start a family
7. take care of your children
8. get divorced
9. look after your parents
10. become a senior citizen
11. die

2 Lösungsvorschlag

My grandfather was born on a farm. He started school at the age of six but he never became a student. He got married to my grandmother, who was named Emma, at the age of 26. They worked together on his farm and waited three years before they started a family. They had two children, my father and my aunt and they took very good care of them. My grandmother told me that they never thought about getting divorced. Now my father and mother look after their parents who are all senior citizens. They enjoy life and I hope they are not going to die for a long time.

107 In hospital (Krankheit)

Bei einigen Wörtern in diesem Brief sind die Buchstaben verdreht. Bringe sie in die richtige Reihenfolge.

Dear Jessie,

Just a note to let you know I can't come and see you next week. I'm afraid I'm in hospital.

I (juinred) _injured_ my knee, and had to have an (paorionte) ______________. No (nboes) ______________ were broken, but the (snik) ______________ and (lusmec) ______________ were in bad shape. And unfortunately, this is a part of the (byod) ______________ that doesn'n (hela) ______________ very quickly. At night I have quite a bit of pain, and it's difficult to (flal laseep) ______________. They gave me a (prcresiption) ______________ for sleeping pills, and that's some help, but I wake up in the morning with a terrible (haceadhe) ______________. But I shouldn't complain. My problem is still relatively harmless. There's a kid in the same room with me who is (geffsirun) ______________ from a fatal illness. I feel so sorry for him.

I hope I (etg bteter) ______________ in time for the big Christmas party at the club. Maybe we'll see each other then.

Best regards,

Audrey

injured
operation
bones
skin
muscle
body
heal
fall asleep
prescription
headache
suffering
get better

Das Datum von heute __________

108 In your spare time
(Befindlichkeiten und Eigenschaften)

1 Hurra, du hast Ferien. Was würdest du gerne tun oder wie würdest du gerne sein? Mache einen Kreis um die Begriffe, die du dir ausgewählt hast.

get sunburned – get suntanned – be healthy – be sick – throw up –

vomit – have the flu – have an upset stomach – become seasick –

become homesick – have a cough – starve – be hungry – laugh –

ignore work – dance – swim – play cards

2 Suche die sechs verborgenen Adjektive. Sie treffen alle auf dich zu und passen in den folgenden Satz.

f	r	g	a	f	i	r	s	t	–	c	l	a	s	s	a	r	z
i	b	r	i	l	l	i	a	n	t	a	p	o	c	l	n	e	o
e	l	e	x	c	e	l	l	e	n	t	u	t	m	y	f	p	k
n	h	a	s	p	l	e	n	d	i	d	a	x	e	b	s	o	g
s	a	t	d	j	p	w	m	a	r	v	e	l	l	o	u	s	v

____

____

____

What are you like? What kind of English learner are you?

You are a(n) ______________________ English learner, but not very modest!

1 Lösungsvorschlag
get sun-tanned – be healthy – laugh – ignore work – dance – swim – play cards

2 first-class – brilliant – excellent – splendid – marvellous – great
YOU are a(n) *excellent* – *brilliant* – *first-class* – *splendid* – *marvellous* – *great* English learner, but not very modest.

V
7/8

Das Datum von heute __________

109 Professions (Berufe)

1 Wer hat das gesagt? Verbinde die Sätze mit den passenden Berufen.

clerk – ambulance man – firefighter – playwright – park ranger – musician

__________________________ Is my guitar in tune?

__________________________ I'll look it up in the files.

__________________________ My next one will be better than Hamlet!

__________________________ An accident on the motorway? We're on our way!

__________________________ The Wilderness Trail begins two miles up that road.

__________________________ We were there because there was an explosion at the gas works.

2 Bilde aus diesen Nomen Berufsbezeichnungen.

1 science __________________________

2 music __________________________

3 build __________________________

4 labour __________________________

5 law __________________________

6 cartoon __________________________

7 crafts __________________________

8 art __________________________

9 manage __________________________

V 7/8

1 musician – clerk – playwright – ambulance man – park ranger – firefighter

2 1 scientist
2 musician
3 builder
4 labourer
5 lawyer
6 cartoonist
7 craftsman
8 artist
9 manager

Das Datum von heute __________

110 Job advertisement (Stellenanzeige)

1 Hier ist eine typische englische Stellenanzeige. Ergänze den Text mit den Wörtern:

creatively – experience – earn – company – skills – hard-working – reliable – independently

Would you like to __________ a dream salary?

Do you enjoy working __________ and __________?

Have you had at least 5 year's __________ in business management?

Our __________ is hiring __________ and __________ experts to do market research.

Computer __________ are absolutely necessary.

Welche Wörter des Textes haben eine ähnliche Bedeutung wie die folgenden?

wages • firm • investigation • abilities • employing • specialists

2 Bringe die Buchstaben in die richtige Reihenfolge.

Scotland Yard is looking for detectives who are

ubsy __________

recaful __________

pctiracal __________

torhghuo __________

ogod at oanirgzing __________

2 busy – careful – practical – thorough – good at organizing

specialists	experts
employing	hiring
abilities	skills
investigation	(market) research
firm	company
wages	salary

1 earn – independently – creatively – experience – company – reliable – hard-working – skills

V 7/8

Das Datum von heute ____________

111 Puzzle (Kreuzworträtsel Berufe)

1 The m____ is very important in city administration.
2 A g____ grows fruit and vegetables.
3 An e____ gives people work.
4 A r____ at a company or hotel answers the telephone and takes care of guests.
5 If you murder someone there's a good chance you will meet a j____.
6 Most people r____ at the age of 65.
7 If you haven't got a job you are____.
8 An a____ plans and designs buildings.
9 A job on an o____ r____ in the North Sea is very lonely but well-paid.
10 An engineer must often know how to r____.
11 … and i____ machines.
12 The opposite of advantage: ____.
13 A s____ works in the field of science.
14 Thomas Edison was a famous i____.
15 The people who number 3 hires are the e____.
16 A j____ interviews people and finds stories for the news.

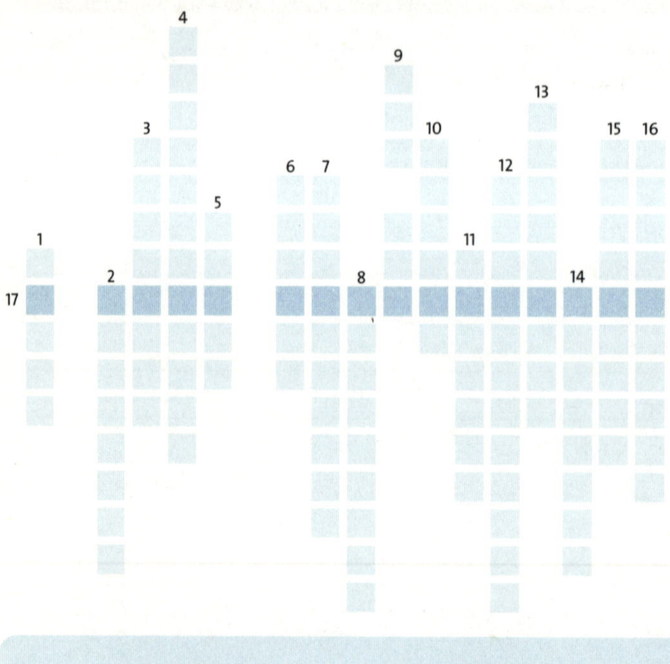

1 mayor
2 gardener
3 employer
4 receptionist
5 judge
6 retire
7 unemployed
8 architect
9 oil-rig
10 repair
11 install
12 disadvantage
13 scientist
14 inventor
15 employees
16 journalist

Lösungswort: A good imagination

V 7/8

Das Datum von heute __________

112 Experience (Verbformen)

1 Fragen zu Erfahrungen in der Vergangenheit werden oft mit dem *present perfect*, das heißt *has/have* mit dem *past participle* gebildet. Ergänze das *past participle* der folgenden Verben.

Have you ever …

1 work: __________ abroad

2 sing: __________ in a choir

3 be: __________ to Rome

4 teach: __________ children

5 buy: __________ a computer

6 feel: __________ ill on a boat

7 meet: __________ a famous person

8 go: __________ hiking in the Alps

9 find: __________ money on the street

10 say: __________ 'I love you.'

11 tell: __________ a riddle

12 make: __________ a bookcase

13 swim: __________ in the Pacific

14 leave: __________ your wallet on a bus

Welche Fragen kannst du mit "Yes, I have!" beantworten?

2 Ergänze den Satz.
Who earns wages without ever doing a day's work?

A _ _ _ _ _   _ _ _ _ _ _ _ _ .

1 1 worked
2 sung
3 been
4 taught
5 bought
6 felt
7 met
8 gone
9 found
10 said
11 told
12 made
13 swum
14 left

2 A night watchman

V 7/8

Das Datum von heute ___________

113 Foreign travel (Reisen)

Schaue dir die drei Reiseprospektanzeigen an. Ordne die unten stehenden Begriffe einem der drei Reiseziele zu.

campsite • ponies • trails • trail guide • campfire • canoe • go fishing • rock-climbing • go orienteering • pack a rucksack • golf course • tennis courts • scuba diving • go sailing • go water-skiing • visit museums • go for a walk • attend concerts • reserve a bed and breakfast or youth hostel • pavement/sidewalks • by charter flight • by train • the most expensive • the cheapest • postcard of the Eiffel Tower • your passport • your national ID

1

Hiking Tours
in the US National Parks
3 or 5 days
with our wilderness experts.
Call Joe or Sally at Adventure Travel,
1–800 735–4680

____
____
____
____
____

2

Need a break?
Try our **3-day**
Get-Away Special
to **Paris!**
from £ 99.– British Rail

____
____
____
____
____

3

"The best 'everything-included' package around."
Fun in the sun for the whole family!
Club Crusoe
five beach locations in Thailand
children under 12 years pay only half-price

____
____
____
____
____

V 7/8

1 campsite – ponies – trails – trail guide – campfire – canoe – go fishing – rock-climbing – go orienteering – pack a rucksack – the cheapest
2 visit museums – go for a walk – attend concerts – reserve a bed and breakfast or youth hostel – pavement/sidewalks – by train – postcard of the Eiffel Tower – your national ID
3 golf course – tennis courts – scuba diving – go sailing – go water skiing – by charter flight – your passport – the most expensive

Das Datum von heute __________

114 Which town? (Reisen und Transport)

Shirley hat in einer anderen Stadt zu tun. Ihre Kollegen haben ihr eine Wegbeschreibung gegeben, wie sie am besten vom Hotel zu ihnen kommt.
Schaue dir die Beschreibungen im Kasten an. Dann ergänze die Sätze mit den passenden Begriffen.
Kannst du erkennen, für welche Stadt sie sind? Überlege, ob die Anweisungen für den Weg zu Fuß, mit öffentlichem Nahverkehr oder für eine Autofahrt sind.

> just opposite the bus stop, number 27 • $1.50 • every ten minutes • to a # 79 bus • a # 1 or # 9 subway uptown • Metrocard or token, no tickets here! • at the 5th stop, that's Madison Ave • go through Central Park, in the direction of the East Side

1 Buy a ______________________

2 The fare is ______________________

3 Take ______________________

4 At 79th Street transfer ______________________

5 You need to ______________________

6 The buses run ______________________

7 Get off the bus ______________________

8 Our Office is ______________________

Wie heißt die Stadt? ______________________

Wie kommt Shirley in das Büro? ______________________

1 1 … Metrocard or token, no tickets here!
2 … $1.50.
3 … a # 1 or # 9 subway.
4 … to a # 79 bus.
5 … go through central Park, in the direction of the East Side.
6 … every ten minutes.
7 … at the 5th stop, that's Madison Ave.
8 … just opposite the bus stop number 27.
New York
By bus and subway.

V
7/8

Das Datum von heute ___________

115 Puzzle (Reisen und Transport)

Waagerecht

1 A person who rides on a train, plane, or other public transport.
4 He had a little of this and ____ in her suitcase.
6 Don't turn right or left. Walk ____ ahead.
7 How can I ____ to the hospital from here?
9 I'd like to travel ____ Bournemouth.
10 When is the return flight? = When is the flight ____?
11 Don't go in there. The sign says ____ ____
12 In a car, the place where you put the suitcases is the ____ in Britain.
13 You must use a ____ in the car to protect yourself from injury.
16 Abbreviation forTechnical University.
18 Another word for a trip.
19 You can park your car in the _____.
21 He stayed ____ his sister's on holiday.
22 It's so close that we can ___ .
23 Just walk ____ that street over there.

Senkrecht

1 The train leaves from ____ 13.
2 I hope we'll get there ____ time.
3 You can fly from the airport to the city centre by ____.
5 When's the next bus ____ Liverpool?
8 You can buy an underground ____ in that machine.
12 How many ____ are there across the Thames?
14 I know where it's going to, but I don't know where it's coming ____.
15 I got ____ because I didn't have a map.
16 Can you ____ me how to get to Trafalgar Square, please?
17 How ____ is it? About 30 miles.
20 At the ____ of the street, turn right.

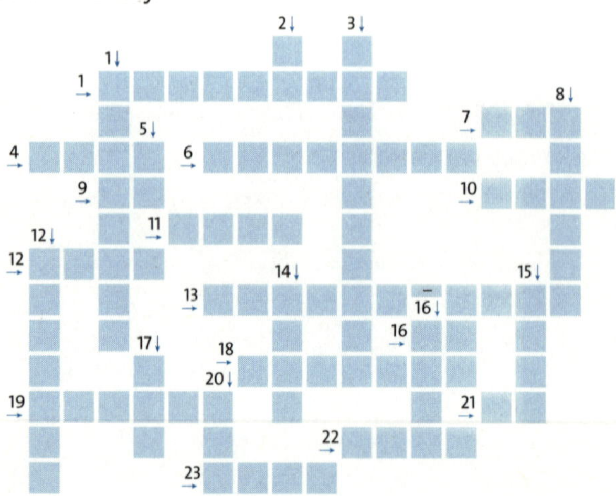

Waagerecht
1 passenger
4 that
6 straight
7 get
9 to
10 back
11 keep
12 boot
13 safety belt
16 TU
18 journey
19 garage
21 at
22 walk
23 down

Senkrecht
1 platform
2 in
3 helicopter
5 to
8 ticket
12 bridges
14 from
15 lost
16 tell
17 far
20 end

V 7/8

Das Datum von heute __________

116 Timetable (Schulfächer)

Schreibe deinen Stundenplan auf Englisch. Schaue im Wörterbuch nach, wenn du bei den Vokabeln Hilfe brauchst.

Hours	Monday	Tuesday	Wednesday	Thursday	Friday
8.00 – 8.45					
8.50 – 9.35					
9.55 – 10.40					
10.45 – 11.30					
11.35 – 12.20					
14.00 – 14.45					
14.50 – 15.35					
15.40 – 16.25					

117 To all students! (Schule)

Suche für die farbigen Begriffe die passende Definition oder Übersetzung aus dem Kasten.

To all students at Elm Street School!
This year we are pleased that school facilities [1] will again be available for a variety of extra-curricular activities between 4.30 and 6 pm. Please remember that adequate grades [2] in your regular school subjects [3] should be a pre-requisite for participation in all extra activities. It has been requested that we give again a list of activites and the teachers who have volunteered [4] to act as advisors [5]. Please contact the individual teachers for further information about time and place.

School play [6] (Nov – Dec and April – May), Ms Winthrop
School newspaper, Ms Jonas
Choir [7], marching band [8] (Sep – Nov), Mr Thorne
Debate Club, Mr Thomas
Writer's Club, Ms Saddleton

Those interested in after-school sports should contact Mr Renton and Mr Whitmore
Approximate starting dates for practice:

Football [9], end August
Soccer [10], end August
Basketball [11], October
Gymnastics [12], November
Wrestling [13], November
Track and field [14], March

Wishing an enjoyable school year!

- **A** to work of your own free will with no pay
- **B** rooms and equipment
- **C** people who give advice
- **D** what you study and learn at School, e. g. maths
- **E** marks given for school work
- **F** a theatre drama performed by pupils
- **G** a group of people who sing together
- **H** musicians with brass instruments who play while marching for parades or sports events
- **I** Ringen
- **J** Leichtathletik
- **K** Turnen
- **L** amerikanischer Fußball
- **M** europäischer Fußball
- **N** Basketball

1 B, 2 E, 3 D, 4 A, 5 C, 6 F, 7 G, 8 H, 9 L, 10 M, 11 N, 12 K, 13 I, 14 J

118 A good student (Lernen)

1 Umkreise die zehn Schulfächer, die hier verborgen sind.

E	R	M	N	O	I	T	A	C	U	D	E		S	U	O	I	G	I	L	E	R
C	O	M	Z	G	E	O	G	R	A	P	H	Y	A	E	N	G	L	I	S	H	A
L	E	D		F	O	I	N	U	N	O	I	C	H	E	M	I	S	T	R	Y	L
C	O	M	P	U	T	E	R		S	T	U	D	I	E	S	H		O	N	S	A
A	P	H	Y	S	I	C	A	L		E	D	U	C	A	T	I	O	N	E	U	T
R		B	I	O	L	O	G	Y	G	F	U	N	X	D	K	L	E	T	A	N	I
T	A	E	C	B	O	N	A	T	O	B	Z	P	H	Y	S	I	C	S	E	Z	N

2 Schreibe die Begriffe in den passenden Kasten. A good student …

complete assignments – try – concentrate – satisfactory – absent often – pay attention – improve – pass – fail – lazy – hard-working – copy test answers – drop out – misunderstand – achieve – goals – get expelled – continue learning

is	does

3 Suche im Kasten oben nach Synonymen für die folgenden Begriffe:

get better – mix something up – reach – focus – finish – carry on

isn't	doesn't

1 GEOGRAPHY – ENGLISH – LATIN – CHEMISTRY – COMPUTER STUDIES – PHYSICAL EDUCATION – BIOLOGY – PHYSICS – ART – RELIGIOUS EDUCATION (auch von rechts nach links suchen)

2 Is: satisfactory – hard working
Does: complete assignments – try – concentrate – pay attention – improve – pass – achieve goals – continue learning
Isn't: absent often – lazy
Doesn't: fail – copy test – answers – drop out – misunderstand – get expelled

3 Synonyme:
get better – improve; mix sth up – misunderstand; reach – achieve goals; focus – concentrate; finish – complete assignments; carry on – continue learning

Das Datum von heute __________

119 A good teacher (Schule und Lernen)

1 Was macht gute Lehrer/innen aus?
Verbinde die Begriffe, damit du sagen kannst, welche Aufgaben sie haben.

A good teacher …

hands out
explains
has enough pieces of
corrects
makes creative & educational
assigns a fair
knows how to turn on
gets to class

on time
wall displays
the meanings of words
chalk
amount of homework
the overhead projector
your pronunciation
worksheets and books

2 Tom hatte gerade seine Hausaufgabe bekommen, als es anfing zu regnen. Hier sind die fehlenden Wörter. Kannst du ihm helfen und sie an der passenden Stelle einfügen?

theme – discuss – excerpt – out – loud – by heart – essay – fiction – climax – character – whole – poem – similar

1 Read the __________ text.

2 Decide: what is the __________ of the story? What is the __________.
Be prepared to __________ your opinion in class.

3 Choose an __________ of 5 to 10 lines of the text to read __________ __________ in class. (10 extra points if you learn it and say it __________ __________.

4 Have you ever felt like the main __________ of the story, or have you ever had a __________ experience? Write a short __________ (15 lines) or __________ (50 lines) about that feeling or event.
It can be fact or __________.

V 7/8

1 A good teacher …
– explains the meaning of words
– corrects your pronunciation
– has enough pieces of chalk
– hands out worksheets and books
– knows how to turn on the overhead projector
– gets to class on time
– makes creative & educational wall displays
– assigns a fair amount of homework

2 1 whole
2 theme – climax – discuss
3 excerpt – out loud – by heart
4 character – similar – poem – essay – fiction

Das Datum von heute __________

120 Four elements (Natur)

Schreibe die Namen der vier Elemente über die vier Blöcke.
Ordne die Begriffe dem passenden Element zu. Dann überlege dir mindestens drei englische Wörter, an die du im Zusammenhang mit den Elementen denkst.

ice – smoke – sandy – wave – atmosphere – desert – quake – get wet – get dry – flood – sticks and twigs – freeze – burn – warmth

water ______________________ a ______________________

e ______________________ f ______________________

water – air – earth – fire

water: wave – get wet – flood – ice – freeze
earth: sandy – desert – quake – sticks and twigs
air: atmosphere – get dry – freeze
fire: smoke – burn – warmth

Lösungsvorschlag: rain – storm – hot – cold

121 Handymen (Technik)

Schreibe die Übersetzungen aller farbigen Begriffe in dieser Anzeige auf.
Übersetze sie dann wieder zurück ins Englische.
Dann finde fünf Werkzeugwörter im Werkzeugkoffer und rahme sie ein.

Calling all handymen and -women

Construct and install your own solar energy system for your house. Get enough electricity to run your fridge,TV, computer, hi-fi and a lot of other electronic equipment. No more worries about a blackout when the city turns on its airconditioning next summer. Let the sun and yourself be your main source of energy, even on dark days and in the romantic moon-light.

a	d	g	t	z	j	l	l	m	o	f
s	c	r	e	w	d	r	i	v	e	r
a	e	h	r	w	p	u	b	s	y	t
w	s	a	i	x	s	c	r	e	w	s
t	r	m	o	a	h	e	n	n	l	u
j	q	m	t	u	t	a	p	a	q	p
f	u	e	t	i	d	n	n	i	k	l
k	a	r	s	f	w	z	o	l	d	g
v	b	o	a	r	d	s	i	s	c	y

____

____

____

____

____

____

____

____

____

____

____

construct: errichten
install: anschließen
energy: Energie
electricity: Elekrizität
to run: betreiben
electronic equipment: elektronische Ausrüstung
blackout: Stromausfall

air-conditioning: Klimaanlage
source of energy: Energiequelle
dark: dunkel
moonlight: Mondlicht

screwdriver – saw – screws – hammer – nails

Das Datum von heute __________

122 Ten terms (Natur)

Suche für die zehn Begriffe die passende Übersetzung aus dem Kasten.

urgent – destroy – land – crop – procedure – grove – consequences – glaciers – acre – upset

1 Folgen ______________________________

2 Vorgang ______________________________

3 zerstören ______________________________

4 Gehölz ______________________________

5 Boden ______________________________

6 0.405 Hektar ______________________________

7 dringend ______________________________

8 durcheinanderbringen ______________________________

9 Gletscher ______________________________

10 Ernte ______________________________

1 consequences
2 procedure
3 destroy
4 grove
5 land
6 acre
7 urgent
8 upset
9 glaciers
10 crop

Das Datum von heute ________

123 Outside (Natur)

Löse das Rätsel und finde das Lösungswort.

1 If it is very s____, you shouldn't go out in a sail boat.

2 I hope it's s____ at the beach tomorrow. I want to get a tan.

3 The trip by ferry was awful. The sea was so r____ .

4 Roses and v____ are my favourite flowers.

5 It's too wet to light the f____ .

6 From the top of the hill you get a wonderful v____ of the countryside.

7 The desert sun is very strong. Don't forget your h____ .

8 Never stand under a tree when there's l____ .

9 You can usually hear this when you see number 8: t____ .

10 He found a new trail through the f___.

11 If you're going to build a campfire, you'd better take some m____ .

12 I need my sunglasses. That sun is so b____ .

13 He loves cities, but I love n____ .

14 Most places are civilized, there isn't much w____ left here.

15 You aren't allowed to h____ deer at this time of year.

16 If you don't have the proper rain gear, you'll g____ w____ .

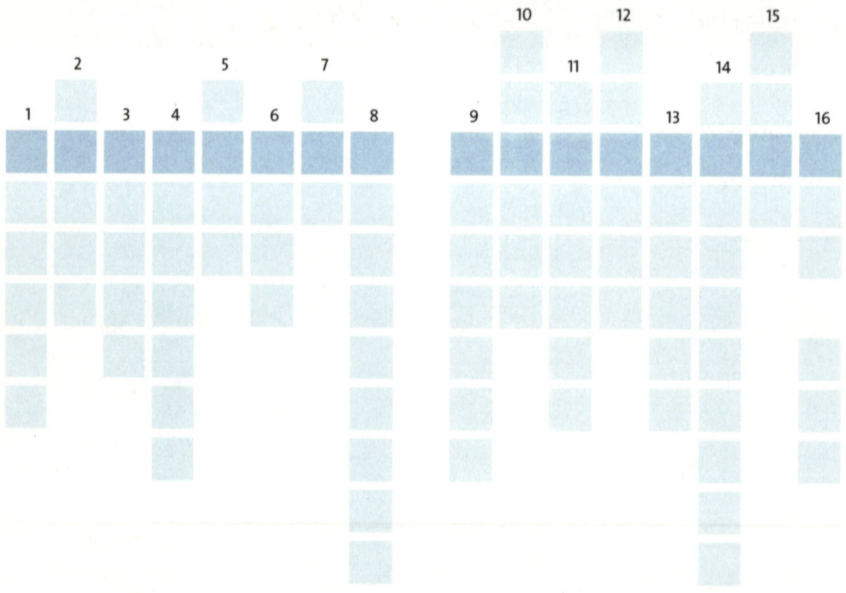

V 7/8

1 stormy
2 sunny
3 rough
4 violets
5 fire
6 view
7 hat
8 lightning
9 thunder
10 forest
11 matches
12 bright
13 nature
14 wilderness
15 hunt
16 get wet
Lösungswort: survival training

Das Datum von heute __________

124 The tropical rain forest (Natur)

Lies diesen Text über Umweltprobleme im tropischen Regenwald und umkreise den zum Satz passenden farbigen Begriff.

In many regions/rooms[1] of the tropical rain forest, pollution/conservation[2] is urgently needed. People there are destroying far too many trees. Sometimes they do this for fuel/fun[3] to heat and cook with. Sometimes the wood is sold, and expensive furniture in the industrialized countries is made/broken[4] of it. But often, thousands of acres of precious forest are simply burned to give poor farmers land to plant/cook[5] and eat/grow[6] their crop. This land is only fertile/frozen[7] for a few years however, and gives the farmers only two or three meals/harvests[8]. The consequences for the earth's climate/diameter[9] are extremely dangerous. Heavenly/Global[10] warming can cause the glaciers to freeze/melt[11] with serious flooding in some parts of the world, and dry land and desserts/deserts[12] in other places. Destroying the earth's rain forests upsets the earth's ecological/economical[13] balance.

Ergänze die Wörter.

How do you feed a tiger?

v__________ c__________________

1 regions
2 conservation
3 fuel
4 made
5 plant
6 grow
7 fertile
8 harvests
9 climate
10 Global
11 melt
12 deserts
13 ecological

very carefully

V 7/8

125 Shopping (Einkaufen)

Schreibe die farbigen Begriffe in die richtige Zeile und dann überlege dir, in welchem Geschäft du die Sachen kaufen kannst. Welches Produkt kannst du in keinem der Geschäfte finden?

I need …			and I could find it in a …
1 a lump of boots	sugar	for my coffee.	supermarket
2 a ton of chili sauce	___________	for the car factory.	___________
3 5 inches of bread	___________	for my jeans patch.	___________
4 a pound of lotion/cream	___________	for the soup.	___________
5 a pair of oranges for	___________	hiking.	___________
6 a tube of meat	___________	for my sunburn.	___________
7 a loaf of ~~sugar~~	___________	for my toast.	___________
8 a can/tin of coal	___________	for the Nachos dip.	___________
9 a bag of material	___________	for the fruit bowl.	___________

department store

supermarket

bakery

butcher's

I need	and I could find it in a …
2 coal	2 none of the shops
3 material	3 department store
4 meat	4 butcher's
5 boots	5 department store
6 lotion	6 department store
7 bread	7 bakery
8 chili sauce	8 supermarket
9 oranges	9 supermarket

Das Datum von heute __________

126 Christmas dinner (essen gehen)

Lies die Geschichte und übersetze die farbigen Wörter ins Deutsche.

My Uncle Alec decided to invite [1] our family to a restaurant for Christmas dinner [2] this year. My mom said that was very generous [3] of him. My Dad said that it was a big surprise because the rest of mom's family was so mean [4]. Anyway, it was a really first class [5] restaurant. When the waiter brought the menu [6] and I saw the high prices [7] I said Uncle Alec would be broke [8] after this. That embarrassed Mom, but Uncle Alec just laughed and asked if he could borrow [9] something from my pocket money [10]. Now, that's a joke! When the waiter came to take our order [11] he said they had run out of [12] peas. Now, that's a stroke of luck. I hate peas. What a great meal [13] it was. Everything tasted [14] delicious. There was roast turkey [15] with a selection [16] of vegetables (except [17] peas), mashed potatoes [18] with gravy [19], Yorkshire pudding, and finally plum pudding for dessert [20]. They brought all the food on big platters or in bowls [21] and we passed them around [22] and helped ourselves [23] – that gave it a homey touch, (in spite of the prices). After we finished eating there was a lot of food left over [24].

____

____

____

____

____

____

____

____

1 invite: einladen
2 dinner: Essen, Abendessen, Festessen
3 generous: großzügig
4 mean: geizig
5 first class: erstklassig
6 menu: Menükarte
7 high prices: hohe Preise
8 broke: pleite
9 borrow: borgen, leihen
10 pocket money: Taschengeld
11 order: Bestellung
12 run out of: ausgehen, zu Ende gehen
13 meal: Mahlzeit, Essen
14 taste: schmecken
15 roast turkey: gebratene Pute
16 selection: Auswahl
17 except: außer
18 mashed potatoes: Kartoffelbrei, Kartoffelpüree
19 gravy: Soße
20 dessert: Nachspeise
21 bowl: Schüssel
22 pass around: herumreichen
23 help oneself: sich selbst bedienen
24 left over: übrig geblieben

Das Datum von heute ___________

127 The blue shirt (Einkaufen)

Bringe die Antworten des Kunden in die richtige Reihenfolge.

1. Here's my driving licence.
2. Yes, please. I'd like to see that shirt over there?
3. Have you got one in medium?
4. No, sorry, not that one. The blue one next to the silk scarf.
5. Then I'll talke large. Can I pay by credit card?

Shop assistant:

a Can I help you?
b This one?
c Here. What size do you need?
d No, sorry, we haven't got any more medium sizes left.
e Of course. Can I see some identification, please.

(a) __ (b) __ (c) __ (d) __ (e) __

Jetzt decke die Antworten des Kunden zu und schaue dir die Sätze des Verkäufers an und versuche, dich an die Antworten des Kunden zu erinnern.

a2 b4 c3 d5 e1

Das Datum von heute ___________

128 Do you like pizza? (Speisen)

1 Schreibe auf Englisch fünf Speisen, die dir gut schmecken, und fünf, die du gar nicht magst.

____

____

____

____

____

2 Schreibe das ganze englische Wort für diese Abkürzungen.

km ____________________

°C ____________________

ft ____________________

kg ____________________

oz ____________________

lb ____________________

gm ____________________

ml ____________________

1 Freie Schüleräußerung

2 km – kilometres
ft – feet
oz – ounces
gm – gram
°C – celsius
kg – kilogram
lb – pound
ml – millilitre

V 7/8

Das Datum von heute __________

129 How high is Mt Everest? (Maße)

Ergänze das fehlende Wort. Dann suche die richtigen Zahlen aus dem Kasten.

–89 • 29,033 • 40,27 • 1000 • 1 • 3,759

1 What's the __________ of Mt Everest? How high is it?

__________ feet.

2 What's the maximum depth of the North Sea?

How __________ is it? __________ feet.

3 What's the __________ of the Panama Canal? How wide is it?

__________ miles.

4 What's the weight of a litre of milk? How much does it __________ ?

__________ kilogram.

5 What's the __________ of the Mississippi River? How long is it?

__________ miles.

6 What's the world's lowest recorded temperature. How __________

was it? __________ °Celsius.

V
7/8

1 height … 29,033 feet
2 deep … 1000 feet
3 width … 40.27 miles
4 weigh … 1 kilogram
5 length … 3,759 miles
6 low … – 89° Celsius

Das Datum von heute __________

130 Communication (Kommunikation)

Diese Sätze stammen aus Gesprächen zwischen zwei Personen. Suche zu jeder Situation das passende Nomen und schreibe auch das passende Verb dazu.

advice – apology – warning – invitation – argument – opinion – request

	Nomen	Verb
1 What a great runner that first girl is! Yes, she's not bad! Poor thing. I feel sorry for her. Yes, so do I.		
2 Oh, dear. I'm terribly sorry! Never mind! It doesn't matter!		
3 If I were in your shoes, I'd see a doctor. You'd better not go swimming. You should get some medicine. You ought to go home.		
4 Would you like to go to Cats with me next friday? I'd love to, but I'm afraid I'm busy then.		
5 Watch out! Be careful! Take care!		
6 I'd like to point out that you didn't signal. You must be joking! I did stop. Now, if you could just calm down!		
7 Could you do me a favour? Would you mind helping me?		

1 opinion; to express an opinion
2 apology; to apologize
3 advice; to advise
4 invitation; to invite
5 warning; to warn
6 argument; to argue
7 request; to request

V 7/8

Das Datum von heute ____________

131 On the phone (Kommunikation)

Löse das große Telefonrätsel.

Senkrecht:

1 He's not here. Can I take a ___?
2 ___ is the Acme Company.
3 Could you give me a ___ tomorrow?
4 I couldn't get through to Mr Smith. The line was ___.
5 This is John Walters ___.
6 Could I ___ a short call from your office, please?
7 A call in this city is a ___ call.
8 A telephone call with a friend is a good chance to get caught up on the latest ___.
9 Some people prefer E-___ to telephoning.
10 The connection was so bad, I'm afraid he didn't hear what I ___.
11 She's not in right now. Please phone ___ after 4 pm.
12 She has a mobile phone, and I have one, ___.

Waagrecht:

7 A call from Munich to Chicago is a ___ call.
9 Is ___ Smith there, please?
13 He's on a business trip. Can I ___ you?
14 The piece of equipment that this puzzle is all about.
15 The US expression for 4 down.
16 Could I ___ you to spell that for me, please.
17 What's the ___ code for Berlin?
18 Where's his telephone number? Have you got ___?
19 ___, I'm afraid I haven't.
20 Even though this fish can be electric, it doesn't usually make telephone calls.
21 Abbreviation for Los Angeles.
22 The line is free now. ___ ahead, Sir!
23 I know she's home. Why doesn't she ___ her phone?

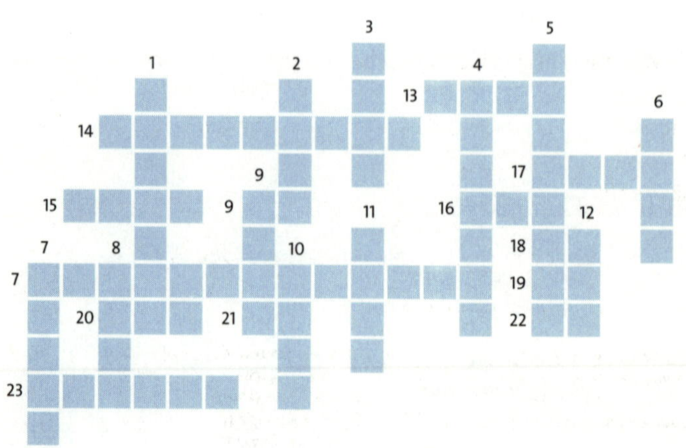

Senkrecht: 1 message 2 this 3 ring 4 engaged 5 speaking 6 make 7 local 8 news 9 mail 10 said 11 back 12 too
Waagrecht 7 long-distance 9 Ms 13 help 14 telephone 15 busy 16 ask 17 area 18 it 19 no 20 eel 21 LA 22 go 23 answer

V 7/8

132 Dear John (Umgangssprache)

Dieser Brief hat viele umgangssprachliche und alltägliche Ausdrücke, die du nicht immer Wort für Wort übersetzen kannst.
Schreibe die deutsche Bedeutung für die farbigen Begriffe obendrüber.

Dear John,

You know how much I care for you. Actually, I thought you were rather fond of me, too. That's why I'm so disappointed that you have let me down again. You really went out with Alice Cooper. I just can't believe it. She has mainly mashed potatoes for brains and she is far from attractive. And she gets on everybody's nerves. Maybe it was her new Super Nintendo that made you do it! However, probably it's all for the best! In a way, we never had much in common anyway. And now this! That's why I believe we should break up! You know, it doesn't really make any difference to me! Probably our relationship was doomed anyway!

By the way, I wonder if Alice will get along with your little sister as well as I did. I'm sure Katie will miss me, even if nobody else does. After all, we're both redheads and Gemini! Say hello to her for me. And keep an eye on her!

Don't ask me to change my mind!

No matter what you do or say, I'll never go out with you again.

care for sb: jdn. mögen
actually: eigentlich, tatsächlich
rather fond of: ziemlich gern haben
that's why: deshalb
let sb down: jdn. enttäuschen
really: wirklich
go out with: ausgehen mit
just: einfach
mainly: vor allem, hauptsächlich
far from: ganz und gar nicht
to get on everybody's nerves: jedermann auf die Nerven gehen
make sb do sth: jdn. dazu bringen, etwas zu tun
however: egal wie
probably: wahrscheinlich
all for the best: nur zum Guten
in a way: in gewisser Weise
in common: gemeinsam
anyway: jedenfalls
that's why: deswegen
break up: auseinandergehen, sich trennen
you know: weißt du
make any difference: irgendeinen Unterschied machen
by the way: übrigens
get along with: auskommen mit
I'm sure: ich bin sicher
after all: schließlich
say hello to: grüßen
keep an eye on: auf jdn. aufpassen
change one's mind: seine Meinung ändern
no matter what: egal was
go out with: ausgehen

Das Datum von heute __________

133 Talk to me (Kommunikation)

1 Diese Wörter haben alle mit Sprechen zu tun. Bringe die Buchstaben in die richtige Reihenfolge.

rcaems ____________________ noma ____________________

lely ____________________ epriwsh ____________________

ohstu ____________________ ksa ____________________

ihsg ____________________ sweran ____________________

2 Streiche die Begriffe durch, die nicht in diesen Satz passen.

apologizes to – respects – annoys – interrupts – joins – complains about – accuses – encourages – supports – compliments – dislikes – turns to – trusts – laughs at – laughs with

A good friend ____________________ you.

1 scream – yell – shout – sigh – moan – whisper – ask – answer

2 Durchzustreichen: annoys – interrupts – accuses – complains about – dislikes – laughs at
A good friend
apologizes to – respects – joins – encourages – supports – compliments – turns to – trusts – laughs with you.

Das Datum von heute ____________

134 Channel six (Fernsehen)

1 Ordne die Programmbeschreibungen der richtigen Fernsehsendung zu.

1 the news ________
2 a chat show ________
3 a film ________
4 a detective series ________
5 a documentary ________
6 a quiz show ________
7 a sports programme ________
8 a music programme ________

Channel six		
1	4.50	Wheel of fortune Players go for a jackpot of £10.000
2	5.30	China: five thousand years of civilization
3	6.30	World football
4	7.00	Top of the Pops
5	8.00	Bandolero Outlaws kill a ranger. With James Stewart and Dean Martin
6	9.30	The Oprah Winfrey Show Interviews with Olympic stars
7	10.30	World News
8	10.40	Columbo A famous actress is dead. Will Columbo find out the truth?

2 Beantworte diese Fragen.

1 Which programmes are more for entertainment?

____

2 Which programmes are more for information?

____

3 Which kind of programme do you enjoy watching best?

____

4 Which of these did you watch last weekend?

____

1 1 7
2 6
3 5
4 8
5 2
6 1
7 3
8 4

2 1 1;3;4;5;6;8
2 2;7
3 Freie Schüleräußerung
4 Freie Schüleräußerung

Das Datum von heute ___________

135 Media (Medien)

Welche Medien würdest du verwenden, um die folgenden Dinge zu finden?

1 the weather report

____

2 today's traffic report

____

3 music

____

4 information for a history project

____

5 a used bicycle to buy

____

6 a good film to watch

____

7 news about your favourite rock group

____

8 a short story

____

9 TV programme listing

____

10 a new friend

____

1 radio, Internet, TV
2 radio
3 radio
4 Internet
5 magazine
6 TV
7 Internet, radio, magazine
8 magazine, radio
9 magazine, newspaper
10 Internet, magazine

Das Datum von heute ___________

136 Was that on the news? (Medien)

1 Finde das Gegenteil und verbinde.

slavery
war
guilty
tragedy

innocent
freedom
comedy
peace

2 Sind diese Sätze falsch oder richtig?

	falsch	richtig	
1 A guilty person is one who has done something wrong.	○	○	___________
2 In a tragedy, the hero or heroine makes you laugh.	○	○	___________
3 It's great to have a holiday in a country where there's a war.	○	○	___________
4  is a symbol for peace.	○	○	___________
5 Charlie Chaplin was a king of comedy.	○	○	___________
6 The Civil War in America stopped freedom for the black population of the south.	○	○	___________
7 Most people enjoy living in slavery.	○	○	___________
8 That criminal is in prison because he is innocent.	○	○	___________

Überall, wo du *falsch* angekreuzt hast, ändere das farbig gedruckte Wort, um den Satzinhalt richtigzustellen.

1 war – peace
slavery – freedom
tragedy – comedy
guilty – innocent

2 1 richtig
2 falsch comedy
3 falsch peace
4 richtig
5 richtig
6 falsch slavery
7 falsch freedom
8 falsch guilty

V 7/8

Das Datum von heute ____________

137 Who is it? (Medien)

1 Welche der farbig gedruckten Begriffe in den Sätzen 1 bis 9 sind die Übersetzungen der Begriffe im Kasten? Schreibe sie hinter die Sätze.

> stehlen – öffentliche Veranstaltung – in die Regierung gewählt – Rechte – Obdachlosenheim – Altersrente – politische und religiöse Gründe – mutig – Herrscher(in)

1. This person wants to be elected in the government. ____________
2. This person is the ruler ____________ of a state, usually by right of birth, but these days with little power.
3. This person has rights ____________ as a member of a country.
4. This person does something courageous. ____________
5. This person hopefully gets an old-age pension. ____________
6. This person is a criminal who robs or steals. ____________
7. This person is sometimes a problem at football matches or other public events. ____________
8. This person has no place to live, but on the street or in a shelter for the homeless. ____________
9. This person has had to leave his/her country for political or religious reasons. ____________

2 Jetzt ordne die Personenbeschreibungen der Nummern 1 – 9 den folgenden Mitgliedern einer Gesellschaft zu.

1 refugee ____________	6 homeless person ____________
2 politician ____________	7 senior citizen ____________
3 hooligan ____________	8 thief ____________
4 citizen ____________	9 king or queen ____________
5 hero(ine) ____________	

V 7/8

1 1 in die Regierung; 2 Herrscher(in); 3 Rechte; 4 mutig; 5 Altersrente; 6 stehlen; 7 öffentliche Veranstaltungen; 8 Obdachlosenheim; 9 politische und religiöse Gründe

2 1 9; 2 1; 3 7; 4 3; 5 4; 6 8; 7 5; 8 6; 9 2

Das Datum von heute ___________

138 Corresponding words
(britisches und amerikanisches Englisch)

Here are some words. Some are British English and some are American English. Look up at least 10 words and put them in the right column. Try to find out the corresponding word for the other column. Look at the examples given!

bobby, bookstore, boot of a car, caravan, chips, cookies, drugstore, elevator (in a house), fall, faucet, flashlight, flat (where you live), garbage, gas, grade (in school), highway, lorry, mailbox, motorway, movie, petrol, purse, rubber, sidewalk, student, subway, timetable, trousers, vacation

British English	American English
lift	elevator
petrol	gas

British English	American English	British English	American English
bobby	cop	motorway	highway
bookshop	bookstore	tap	faucet
boot of a car	trunk of a car	lorry	truck
caravan	trailer	letterbox	mailbox
crisps	chips	film	movie
chips	French fries	handbag	purse
biscuits	cookies	rubber	eraser
chemist's	drugstore	pavement	sidewalk
autumn	fall	pupil	student
torch	flashlight	underground	subway
flat	apartment	timetable	schedule
rubbish	garbage	trousers	pants
mark	grade	holidays	vacation

Das Datum von heute __________

139 Working with a dictionary (amerikanisches Englisch)

What do American people mean when they say the following sentences?
Read the sentences and choose the right explanations.

1 I always go on holiday in fall.
(a) This person always goes on holiday by plane. **(b)** This person always goes on holiday in autumn. **(c)** This person always goes on holiday after he has had an accident.

2 The book is in the trunk.
(a) The book is in one of the person's suitcases. **(b)** The book is in the elephant house. **(c)** The book is in the back part of a car.

3 The student is 14 years old.
(a) The 14-year-old is at the university. **(b)** The 14-year-old is at school. **(c)** The 14-year-old has left school.

4 Where is the flashlight?
(a) This person wants to light a candle. **(b)** This person wants to turn on the lights in his car. **(c)** This person wants to light up his way in the dark.

5 I'm going to a movie tomorrow.
(a) This person is moving into a new house tomorrow.
(b) This person is going to go somewhere by car tomorrow.
(c) This person is going to go to the cinema tomorrow.

6 I have lost my purse.
(a) This person has lost the thing in which she puts her money. **(b)** This person has lost her handbag. **(c)** This person has lost her shopping bag.

V
7/8

1b
2c
3b
4c
5c
6b

140 Indians (Nordamerika)

1 The Indians called the white people _ _ _ _ faces.

2 The modern name for Indians is _ _ _ _ _ _ _ _ Americans.

3 The European settlers landed with their ships at the _ _ _ _ coast of America.

4 People went west and hoped to find _ _ _ _ and get rich.

5 The settlers who came to North America first are often called the

_ _ _ _ _ _ _ _ .

6 At first the Indians liked the settlers but then they started to _ _ _ _ them because they took their lands away from them.

7 The white man told the Indians to live in special areas called

_ _ _ _ _ _ _ _ _ _ _ _ .

8 Gold was found in the _ _ _ _ of America.

9 A lot of settlers had these animals because of their milk: _ _ _ _ .

10 An Indian tent is called a _ _ _ _ _ .

11 The Indians used the _ _ _ _ of animals to make shoes.

12 The Apaches are an Indian _ _ _ _ _ .

13 In Hollywood films an Indian woman is called a _ _ _ _ _ .

14 Today Indians do not have to _ _ _ _ in reservations.

1 pale
2 Native
3 east
4 gold
5 pioneers
6 hate
7 reservations
8 west
9 cows
10 tepee
11 skin
12 tribe
13 squaw
14 live

V
7/8

Das Datum von heute ____________

141 Das simple present

Schau dir die Tabelle an und dann beantworte die Fragen.

	The Bunns	Charley	Diana
Monday evening	go bowling (always)	play cards (usually)	clean her room (never)
Wednesday evening	work in the garden (sometimes)	watch TV (always)	practise guitar (always)
Friday evening	visit friends (usually)	read his comics (sometimes)	meet her friends (usually)
Saturday evening	do the shopping (never)	sleep until midday (sometimes)	help in a shop (always)
Sunday	have visitors (sometimes)	do his homework (never)	make breakfast (usually)

1 What do the Bunns do on Sundays?

The Bunns <u>sometimes have visitors</u> on Sundays.

2 When does Diana clean her room?

Diana ________________ her room on Monday evenings.

3 Do the Bunns go bowling on Saturdays?

No, they ________________ bowling on Monday evenings.

4 Does Diana always go to the cinema on Fridays?

No, she ________________ her friends on Fridays.

5 Does Charley play cards on Wednesday evening?

No, he ________________ TV on Wednesday evenings.

6 Do the Bunns always eat in a restaurant on Fridays?

No, they ________________ on Fridays.

7 When does Charley get up on Saturdays?

Charley ________________ on Saturdays.

8 What does Diana do when she gets up on Sundays?

She ________________.

G 7/8

2 never cleans
3 always go
4 usually meets
5 always watches
6 usually visit friends
7 sometimes sleeps until midday
8 usually makes breakfast on Sundays

Das Datum von heute __________

142 Fragen mit simple present

Bilde Fragen, indem du nach den unterstrichenen Satzteilen fragst.

1 Mr Bunn works at night.

When does Mr Bunn work? __________ ?

2 Charley enjoys going for long walks in the woods.

What __________ doing?

3 On Monday evenings Diana goes to night school *(Abendschule)*.

__________ Diana __________ to night school?

4 Thousands of tourists go skiing in the Alps.

__________ thousands of tourists __________ ?

5 Colin can't play in the match because he has broken his leg.

__________ in the match?

6 Alison collects flower books. She's got nearly a hundred now.

__________ flower books __________ ?

7 Mr Hudd always goes to Wales in August.

__________ to Wales in August?

2 does Charley enjoy … ?
3 When does … go … ?
4 Where do … go skiing?
5 Why can't Colin play … ?
6 How many … has Alison got?
7 Who always goes … ?

G 7/8

143 Das simple past

Hier ist Glorias Terminkalender für letzte Woche.
Schreibe auf, was sie alles getan hat.

Monday 4 p. m., go to dentist	Friday 6.30 p. m., practise for swimming match
Tuesday buy birthday present for Uncle Bob	Saturday 10 a. m., meet Gilda at café
Wednesday 5.15 p. m., have piano lesson	Sunday afternoon, prepare for English test
Thursday visit Aunt Mabel in hospital	

1 On Monday Gloria went to the dentist at four o'clock.

2 On Tuesday she ____________________ for Uncle Bob.

3 On Wednesday she ____________________ at a quarter past five.

4 She ____________________ in hospital on Thursday.

5 She ____________________ at 6.30 p.m. on Friday.

6 On Saturday Gloria ____________________ at the café at ten o'clock.

7 Gloria ____________________ on Sunday afternoon.

G 7/8

2 bought a birthday present
3 had a piano lesson
4 visited Aunt Mabel
5 practised for the swimming match
6 met Gilda
7 prepared for the English test

Das Datum von heute __________

144 Simple present oder simple past?

Benutze die unten angegebenen Verben, um diesen Text über Bobs Cousine Alison zu vervollständigen. Überlege dabei, ob du das *simple present* oder das *simple past* verwenden musst.

be *(2 x)* – buy – drive – get – go – have *(3 x)* – not have – live *(4 x)* – move – rent – say – tell – think – want – work

Now Alison ______________ [1] in London and ______________ [2] for a big bank. She ______________ [3] to London last year. Before that, she ______________ [4] in Glasgow. She ______________ [5] to school in Glasgow, and ______________ [6] her first job there, too.

Her parents still ______________ [7] in Scotland. Alison ______________ [8] a small flat in Glasgow, but now she ______________ [9] just one small room in a poor part of London.

She ______________ [10] that life in London ______________ [11] much more expensive than it ______________ [12] in Glasgow.

But Alison ______________ [13] a nice little car now. She ______________ [14] it last month. She often ______________ [15], "Last year I ______________ [16] a lovely flat, but I ______________ [17] a car. This year, I ______________ [18] a car, but I ______________ [19] in one little room." She ______________ [20] her parents that next year she ______________ [21] to have a nice flat and a nice car.

1 lives
2 works
3 moved
4 lived
5 went
6 got
7 live
8 had
9 rents
10 thinks
11 is
12 was
13 drives
14 bought
15 says
16 had
17 didn't have
18 have
19 live
20 tells (told)
21 wants

Das Datum von heute ____________

145 Aussagesätze, Fragen und verneinte Sätze mit *simple present* und *simple past*

In dieser gemischten Übung von Aussagesätzen, Fragen und verneinten Sätzen musst du zwischen *simple present* und *simple past* unterscheiden. Setze die angegebenen Verben in die Sätze ein.

1 Miss Jolly ________________ (go) to the seaside every weekend during the summer.

2 Mark only ________________ (learn) to swim last year and today he ________________ (be) the best swimmer in the school. I ________________ (not be) surprised. He ________________ (practise) every day. He ________________ (never do) anything else.

3 Bob often ________________ (help) at home. He ________________ (like) cooking. Last Christmas when his mum ________________ (be) in hospital he even ________________ (make) the Christmas dinner.

4 Mum, why ________________ (Tom/always/wear) my best T-shirts? Yesterday he ________________ (take) my red one and this morning he ________________ (have) my new blue one on. Why ________________ (you/not buy) him some?

1 goes
2 learnt – is – 'm not – practises – never does
3 helps – likes – was – made
4 does Tom always wear …? – took – has – don't you buy …?

Das Datum von heute ___________

146 Kreuzworträtsel mit Zeiten

Um das Kreuzworträtsel zu lösen, musst du bei jedem Satz ein sinnvolles Verb einsetzen. Achte dabei besonders auf die Zeitangaben.

Across

1 At weekends the children often ____ cards with their parents.
5 Have you all ____ your English books with you?
6 Yesterday my father ____ us to school because we missed the bus.
7 What's for tea? I ____ always very hungry after sport.
8 I ____ a very exciting film on TV last night.
10 I can't come and see you on Sunday. We always ____ my uncle then.
13 Mrs Clarke ____ us jokes at the end of the lesson.
15 My dad has to ____ in the afternoons because he works at night.
18 You've got a bad cold. Why don't you ____ some medicine?

Down

1 Brenda plays the piano well. She ____ for two hours every day.
2 If you ____ two and two, you get four.
3 Jim always ____ across the road instead of waiting for the green man.
4 Mrs Bunn ____ the shopping on her way home from work.
5 Our neighbours are horrible. They often ____ their poor little dog.
9 David ____ his car every Saturday.
11 Alison ____ a very good pianist.
12 Don't ____ late again, or you will have to stay after school.
14 John ____ school when he was 16.
16 Don't ____ too many toffees. They are bad for your teeth.
17 You can look round the shops by yourselves now, and we will all ____ at the bus in two hours. Don't be late.

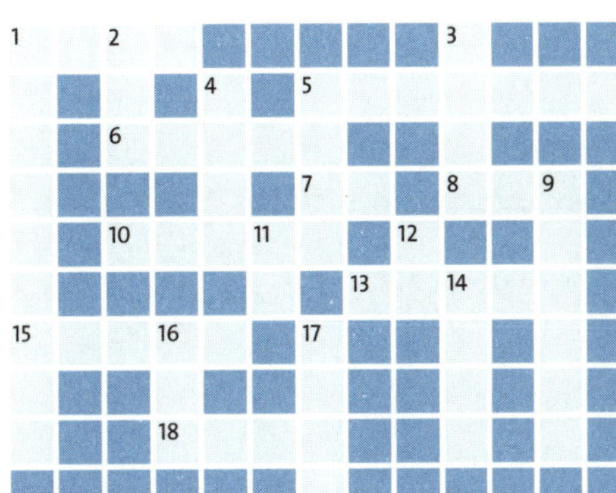

Across
1 play
5 brought
6 drove
7 am
8 saw
10 visit
13 tells
15 sleep
18 take

Down
1 practises
2 add
3 runs
4 does
5 beat
9 washes
11 is
12 be
14 left
16 eat
17 meet

G 7/8

Das Datum von heute __________

147 Das present perfect mit for/since I

1 Sind die folgenden Zeitangaben „Zeiträume“ oder „Zeitpunkte“? Schreibe je nachdem *for* bzw. *since* dazu.

1 __________ ten o'clock
2 __________ Christmas
3 __________ last summer
4 __________ ten minutes
5 __________ one month
6 __________ the last lesson
7 __________ a long time
8 __________ a week
9 __________ I last saw you
10 __________ the beginning of the term

2 Setze *for* bzw. *since* und die richtige Form des *present perfect* in die Sätze ein.

1 Joe has been (be) at this school for five years.
2 Where's Alison? I __________ (not see) her __________ this morning.
3 Mr Pryce __________ (know) his wife __________ they were both small children.
4 Ben __________ (not see) his uncle __________ several years.
5 I __________ (not be) very well __________ Monday.
6 My brother __________ (have) his new motorbike __________ two weeks.
7 They __________ (live) here __________ they first came to Britain.
8 The poor animal is very hungry. He __________ (not have) anything to eat __________ days.

G 7/8

1 1 since 2 since 3 since 4 for 5 for 6 since 7 for 8 for 9 since 10 since

2 2 haven't seen – since 3 has known – since 4 hasn't seen – for 5 haven't been – since 6 has had – for 7 have lived – since 8 hasn't had – for

Das Datum von heute ___________

148 Das present perfect mit for/since II

Übersetze die Sätze ins Englische.

1 Sie ist seit heute Morgen im Krankenhaus.

____

____!

2 Joe wohnt seit fünf Jahren in Norwich.

____

____

3 Wir kennen uns seit Juni 1985.

____

____

4 – Wie lange bist du schon hier?

____

– Ich bin hier seit einer halben Stunde.

____

5 Ich habe diesen Füller *(fountain-pen)*, seit ich ein Kind war.

____

____

1 She has been in hospital since this morning.
2 Joe has lived in Norwich for five years.
3 We have known each other since June 1985.
4 – How long have you been here?
– I have been here for half an hour.
5 I have had this fountain-pen since I was a child.

G 7/8

Das Datum von heute ___________

149 Simple past oder present perfect?

Setze die angegebenen Verben ein. Benutze das *simple past* bzw. das *present perfect*.

Last year we ______________ [1] (go) to the USA on holiday. We ____________ [2] (fly) to New York. The airport ____________ [3] (be) huge *(riesig)*.

We ___________________ [4] (not walk) along the corridors. There __________ [5] (be) moving walkways to take us from the plane to the customs.

___________________ [6] (you/be) to America before? __________________ [7] (ask) the customs officer.

'Yes, we ____________________ [8] (visit) California five years ago,'

________________________ [9] (reply) my mother.

'How long ____________________ [10] (you/stay) then?'

'We ____________________ [11] (stay) just five weeks,' ___________________ [12] (say) my father.

'___________________ [13] (you/bring) any fresh food, plants or animals with you this time?'

'No, we ____________________ [14] (not bring) anything like that,'

we ____________________ [15] (answer).

1 went
2 flew
3 was
4 didn't walk
5 were
6 Have you been …?
7 asked
8 visited
9 replied
10 did you stay …?
11 stayed
12 said
13 Have you brought …?
14 didn't bring (have not brought)
15 answered

G 7/8

Das Datum von heute ________

150 Das present perfect progressive (Form)

Setze die Verben in die Sätze ein. Benutze durchweg das *present perfect progressive.*

1 Sally has been doing (do) the test for 45 minutes.

2 The sun ________ (shine) since early morning.

3 We ________ (lie) in the garden for three hours.

4 Freddy ________ (learn) his irregular verbs for ten minutes.

5 It ________ (rain) for four days now. What a holiday!

6 Alison and Jack ________ (play) tennis for two hours.

7 The British and the French ________ (talk) about a Channel tunnel since the 18th century.

8 Mrs Pryce ________ (try) to phone her friend in the USA for 30 minutes, but she can't get through.

2 has been shining
3 have been lying
4 has been learning
5 has been raining
6 have been playing
7 have been talking
8 has been trying

Das Datum von heute ___________

151 Das present perfect progressive (Gebrauch)

Übersetze die Sätze ins Englische.

1 Ich stehe hier seit über einer Stunde.

2 Beeil dich! Du spielst mit deinem Essen seit fast einer Stunde.

3 Dominic, du trägst diese Jeans schon seit zwei Wochen.

4 Mr Brown baut sein Haus seit 1986.

5 Die Kinder machen seit Anfang der Stunde Lärm.

6 Joe und Anne räumen ihre Zimmer seit dem Frühstück auf.

G 7/8

1 I have been standing here for more than an /one hour.
2 Hurry up! You have been playing with your food for nearly an / one hour.
3 Dominic, you have been wearing those jeans for two weeks.
4 Mr Brown has been building his house since 1986.
5 The children have been making a noise since the beginning of the lesson.
6 Joe and Ann have been tidying (up) their rooms since breakfast.

152 -ing-Formen

Die *-ing-Formen* der vierzehn angegebenen Verben sind in dem *Lettersquare* versteckt. 3 davon sind normal (→), 4 von oben nach unten (↓), 4 von unten nach oben (↑), und 3 schräg (↙↘) geschrieben. Kannst du die 14 *-ing-Formen* finden?

~~camp~~ – do – drive – fish – garden – laugh – make – play – practise – read – run – swim – talk – wait

P	E	H	I	G	A	G	T	N	G	G	Z	O	T	F
V	A	L	E	N	N	I	L	T	N	H	E	B	A	Q
K	U	I	M	I	P	L	A	Y	I	N	G	R	L	Z
E	G	B	P	K	R	S	U	C	V	S	W	Y	K	P
F	M	M	X	A	A	S	G	D	I	R	C	O	I	Q
S	A	T	W	M	C	L	H	D	R	O	N	X	N	A
C	G	U	S	A	T	F	I	A	D	O	I	N	G	G
C	N	B	W	N	I	X	N	M	D	Y	O	Z	Y	P
A	I	K	I	C	S	T	G	B	J	X	J	M	N	G
W	N	U	M	D	I	L	I	E	H	W	K	Q	N	N
Z	E	K	M	R	N	E	V	N	H	G	S	I	A	I
U	D	E	I	T	G	S	K	P	G	O	H	P	I	N
F	R	V	N	J	V	Q	L	D	F	S	L	X	Q	N
G	A	J	G	U	R	E	A	D	I	N	G	V	B	U
W	G	Y	H	M	I	R	T	F	W	C	N	J	R	R

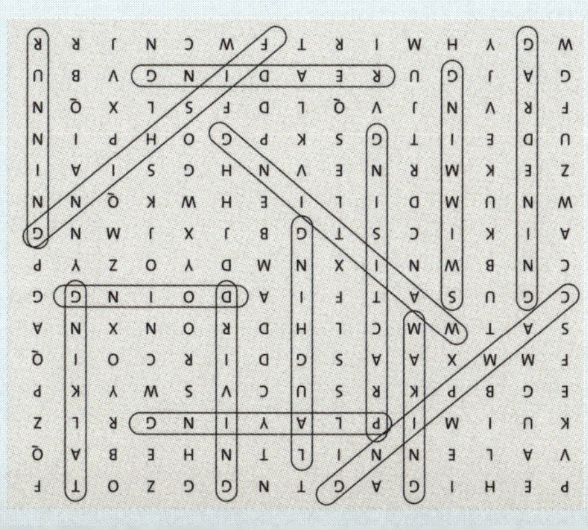

1 camping
2 doing
3 driving
4 fishing
5 gardening
6 laughing
7 making
8 playing
9 practising
10 reading
11 running
12 swimming
13 talking
14 waiting

G 7/8

Das Datum von heute ___________

153 Das *past perfect*

Letzten Monat besuchte Ben Taylor seine alte Schule. Er fand, dass sich inzwischen vieles geändert hatte. Setze die Verben ein. Benutze durchweg das *past perfect*.

1 Mr Havers was no longer there. He had left (leave) the school six years before.

2 When Ben was at the school, they hadn't build (not build) the games room yet.

3 Miss Smith was now Mrs Jones, and Miss Brown, the Maths teacher, had become (become) Mrs Rossi.
They had married (marry) other teachers several years before.

4 Ben's lovely old wooden desk wasn't there any more. The school had bought (buy) new plastic ones.

5 His old classroom was no longer grey. It had been (be) painted green.

6 Ben didn't meet his old form teacher. She had died (die) in 1976.

G 7/8

2 hadn't built
3 had become – had married
4 had bought
5 had been
6 had died

Das Datum von heute ___________

154 Simple past oder past perfect?

Benutze das *simple past* bzw. das *past perfect*. Beachte bei jedem Satz die Reihenfolge der Handlungen.

1 When the ship __sank__ (sink), they __had been__ (be) at sea for a month.

2 After Lenny ________________ (see) a film about Captain Cook, he ________________ (decide) to read a book about him.

3 Anne ______________________________ (never ride) on an elephant before she ________________ (go) to London Zoo.

4 When Captain Scott ________________ (reach) the South Pole he ________________ (find) that the explorer Amundsen ____________________ ________________ (already be) there.

5 When Mrs Cary finally __________ (get) to the bus stop, the bus ____________ ____________________ (already leave).

6 When Mr Gilbert ________________ (look) at the signpost, he ________________ (realize) that he ________________ (take) the wrong road.

7 Mrs Green ________________ (arrive) at the post office at 12.30, but it ________________ (shut) half an hour earlier.

2 had seen – decided
3 had never ridden – went
4 reached – found – had already been
5 got – had already left
6 looked – realized – had taken
7 arrived – had shut

G 7/8

Das Datum von heute ____________

155 Das Futur

Setze die angegebenen Verben ein. Benutze das *going to-future* oder das *will-future*. Denke daran, dass das *going to-future* nur für feste Pläne und Absichten benutzt wird; sonst verwendet man *will.*

1 Bob is having an interview for a job as a bank clerk. I think he will get (get) the job.

2 Colin is buying a ticket to Canada. He ______________________ (fly) there to see his grandparents.

3 Jane has to do a test to get into university. If she's lucky, she ______________ (go) to Cambridge next year.

4 John is looking at the racing bikes in the shop window. He says that one day he ______________________ (buy) a good bike.

5 Young Tim is too short to see the game properly. When he is older he ______________ (be) tall enough to see it.

6 Paula has bought a book on German. She ______________________ (spend) her holidays in Germany this year.

7 Peter is very interested in politics. He hopes one day people ______________ (choose) him to go to Parliament.

8 Ted Brown has passed his driving test. Now he and Philip ______________________ (start) a taxi service.

9 You ______________ (not get) a good job, Brian. You are so lazy.

2 is going to fly
3 will go
4 is going to buy
5 will be
6 is going to spend
7 will choose
8 are going to start
9 won't get

G 7/8

Das Datum von heute ___________

156 Das *present progressive* mit zukünftiger Bedeutung

Die Pengbornes sind immer sehr beschäftigt. Sie tragen ihre Termine in einen gemeinsamen Terminkalender ein. Sieh dir den Kalender an und sage, was die Pengbornes in den nächsten Tagen alles vorhaben. Benutze durchweg das *present progressive* mit einem Adverb der zukünftigen Zeit.

Monday	Julie, have ballet class, 5 p. m.
Tuesday	Jim, practise guitar with Ben, 6.30 Mum, meet Joan for coffee, 3.30 Dad, play in darts match, 7.30
Wednesday	Julie and Jim, attend youth club meeting, 6 Dad, take car to garage, 3 o'clock
Thursday	Hurrah! Today there is nothing to do!
Friday	Julie, help Mum with shopping, after school Dad, pick up Bob Clarke for Golf, 2.15

1 On Monday Julia _is having_ a ballet class _at 5_.

2 On Tuesday Jim ______________ the guitar with Ben ______________, Mrs Pengborne ______________ Joan for coffee ______________ and Mr Pengborne ______________ in a darts match.

3 On Wednesday Julie and Jim ______________ a youth club meeting ______________ and Mr Pengborne ______________ the car to the garage ______________.

4 The Pengbornes ______________ nothing on Thursday.

5 On Friday Julie ______________ Mrs Pengborne with the shopping ______________ and Mr Pengborne ______________ up Bob Clarke for golf ______________.

2 is practising – at 6.30 – is meeting at 3.30 – is playing – at 7.30
3 are attending – at 6 – is taking – at 3
4 are doing
5 is helping – after school – is picking – at 2.15

G 7/8

157 Das simple present mit zukünftiger Bedeutung

Peter und sein Freund Jack planen eine Rundreise durch Europa.
Setze die angegebenen Verben in den Dialog ein. Benutze dabei durchweg das *simple present*.

Peter The train for Dover leaves [1] (leave) London Victoria every hour. We needn't worry. The ferry ______________ [2] (not go) until the train ______________ [3] (arrive).

Jack Fine. And how are we going to get to Cologne?

Peter No problem. Look, there ______________ [4] (be) a train from Ostend to Vienna. It ______________ [5] (stop) at Cologne. It ______________ [6] (go) an hour after the ferry ______________ [7] (get) in, so we'll have plenty of time.

Jack Yes, but that train is a bit expensive, isn't it?

Peter Well, we could go by coach (Reisebus), I suppose.
An express coach __________ [8] (leave) London for Cologne every day at 10 p.m. But it __________ [9] (take) much longer than the train.
It ____________________________ (not reach) Cologne until midday the next day.

2 doesn't (does not) go
3 arrives
4 is
5 stops
6 goes
7 gets
8 leaves
9 takes
10 does not reach

158 Verschiedene Formen des Futurs

Vervollständige die Sätze mit einer passenden Form des Futurs. Nur eine richtige Lösung ist möglich.

1 – What are you going to do (do) when you leave school?

– Oh, I ______________________ (be) a vet, I hope.

2 – Hurry up, Betty. We ________________ (miss) the train. It ________________ (leave) at 10, you know.

– Don't worry. We ______________________ (must take) a taxi to the station then.

3 – I'm afraid I ________________ (cannot come) to an interview next Friday. We ________________ (go) on holiday the next day and I ________________ (help) my mother with the packing.

– You ______________________ (never get) a good job like that!

4 Now you must be very careful with this microscope or it ________________ (break). Then your parents ________________ (get) a bill *(Rechnung)* from the school and they ________________ (must pay) for it to be repaired.

5 The film ________________ (start) at 8, so we ______________________ (meet) in front of the cinema at 7.45. And don't forget that you ________________ (need) £ 2.50 to get in.

1 am going to be
2 will miss – leaves – will have to take
3 cannot come – are going – am helping – will never get
4 will break – will get – must / will have to pay
5 starts – will / are going to meet – will need

Das Datum von heute ___________

159 Question tags mit Hilfsverb

Hänge das *question tag* an die Sätze an. In allen Sätzen gibt es ein Hilfsverb, das du zur Bildung des *question tag* benutzen kannst.

1 Miss Sutherland has just moved from Scotland to America, hasn't she ?

2 Jack, you have been to the USA, ______________________________ ?

3 The Americans don't drive on the left, ______________________________ ?

4 July 4th is Independence Day, ______________________________ ?

5 Texas and California were once Spanish, ______________________________ ?

6 Susan, you shouldn't go on the New York subway *(U-Bahn)* alone at night, ______________________________ ?

7 We can go to a Baseball match on Saturday, ______________________________ ?

8 The Americans are very friendly people, ______________________________ ?

2 haven't you?
3 do they?
4 isn't it?
5 weren't they?
6 should you?
7 can't we?
8 aren't they?

Das Datum von heute ___________

160 Question tags ohne Hilfsverb

Hänge das *question tag* an die Sätze an. In diesen Sätzen gibt es kein Hilfsverb, das du benutzen kannst.

1 People speak English in the USA, don't they ?

2 The Pryces went to Florida last year, ______________________ ?

3 You visited Hollywood, too, ______________________ ?

4 Jack knows quite a lot about the USA, ______________________ ?

5 I get a visa from the US Embassy *(Botschaft)*, ______________________ ?

6 The Navajo lived in Arizona, ______________________ ?

7 We crossed the frontier between the USA and Canada at Emersen in Manitoba,

______________________ ?

8 The shops stay open very late in America, ______________________ ?

2 didn't they?
3 didn't you?
4 doesn't he?
5 don't I?
6 didn't they?
7 didn't we?
8 don't they?

Das Datum von heute ___________

161 Question tags übersetzen

Übersetze die unterstrichenen Satzteile ins Englische.

1 Central Park ist in Manhattan, <u>nicht wahr?</u>

____

2 Amerikanische Kinder bekommen kaum Hausaufgaben, <u>oder?</u>

____

3 Die meisten Amerikaner können Englisch, <u>oder nicht?</u>

____

4 Lola kann nicht mit. Sie hat keine Zeit, <u>oder?</u>

____

5 Fast alle Amerikaner haben ein Auto, <u>nicht wahr?</u>

____

6 Viele Asiaten wohnen in Los Angeles, <u>nicht wahr?</u>

____

7 Neuengland war früher eine britische Kolonie, <u>oder?</u>

____

8 Zunächst halfen die Indianer den Siedlern, <u>nicht wahr?</u>

____

9 Los Angeles und San Francisco waren früher spanische Städte, <u>nicht wahr?</u>

____

G 7/8

1 isn't it?
2 don't they?
3 can't they?
4 has she?
5 haven't they?
6 don't they?
7 wasn't it?
8 didn't they?
9 weren't they?

Das Datum von heute ___________

162 Short answers

Schreibe zu den Sätzen eine geeignete Kurzantwort. Benutze die am Satzende angegebenen Namen. Achte dabei auf die Zeichen: bei ⊞ musst du den angegebenen Satz bejahen; bei ⊟ musst du den angegebenen Satz verneinen.

1 Gerda doesn't understand Spanish. (Maria)

⊟ But Maria does. ___________

2 Jane doesn't want to go to the pyjama party. (we)

⊟ But ___________

3 Marcia hasn't got an invitation to the barbecue. (I)

⊟ ___________

4 Harry forgot to bring some coke. (Wayne)

⊟ ___________

5 Susan didn't go to the hairdresser's. (Alison)

⊞ ___________

6 Jon went to a summer camp in Nevada last summer. (Hank)

⊞ ___________

7 I wasn't invited to the barbecue last year. (they)

⊟ ___________

8 They shouldn't smoke so much. (you)

⊞ ___________

9 Alison got a good grade at school last year. (Gerda)

⊞ ___________

10 Wayne can swim very fast indeed. (Jason)

⊟ ___________

2 (But) we do.
3 But I have.
4 But Wayne didn't.
5 Neither did Alison.
6 So did Hank.
7 But they were.
8 Neither should you.
9 So did Gerda.
10 But Jason can't.

Das Datum von heute ____________

163 So, neither, but

Vervollständige die Sätze mit *so …*, *neither …*, *but …*

1 Those boys are Sioux Indians and ________________ I.

2 New York isn't very clean and ____________________________ Detroit.

3 Lisa can't drive and ___________________________ Sharon.

4 Wayne doesn't know the way to the 'Caesar's Palace' ________________ Grant ________________ .

5 Sharon never goes on the subway alone and _________________________ Lisa.

6 Grant speaks Spanish and ________________ Jeff.

7 Sharon hasn't been at school for two days and ____________________ Wayne.

8 Jeff only got into junior college because he's so good at baseball and ________________ Mike.

9 Grant likes dancing very much ________________ Wayne ________________ .

G 7/8

1 so am
2 neither is
3 neither can
4 but … does
5 neither does
6 so does
7 neither has
8 so did
9 but … doesn't

Das Datum von heute ___________

164 Short answers übersetzen

Übersetze die unterstrichenen Kurzantworten ins Englische.

1 – Lisa liebt Spaghettieis. – Aber ich nicht.

____

2 – Grant wurde nicht in Houston geboren. – Aber ich.

____

3 – Wayne mag keine Hotdogs. – Ich auch nicht.

____

4 – Ich war letztes Jahr in Mexiko. – Martin aber nicht.

____

5 – Ich konnte nicht schwimmen, als ich sechs Jahre alt war. – Wayne auch nicht.

____

6 – Ich habe meinen Führerschein. – Jason aber nicht.

____

7 – Mein Vater arbeitet in Houston. – Lisas Vater auch.

____

8 – Grant wohnt in Dallas. – Wayne aber nicht.

____

1 But I don't.
2 But I was.
3 Neither do I.
4 But Martin wasn't.
5 Neither could Wayne.
6 But Jason hasn't.
7 So does Lisa's father.
8 But Wayne doesn't.

Das Datum von heute ____________

165 Modale Hilfsverben – may, may not, might

Übersetze die unterstrichenen Satzteile ins Deutsche.

1 Don't visit Tim this week. You might catch his cold.

2 Simon may be late. He had to go to the doctor's.

3 You may get up today, but don't get dressed.

The doctor may want to look at you again,

4 May I go to the youth club dance tomorrow?

No, you may not. You still have a temperature *(Fieber)*.

5 May Ann come round this afternoon, Mum?

No, I'm sorry, dear. You might be late for your piano lesson.

G 7/8

1 holst vielleicht / könntest holen
2 hat vielleicht Verspätung
3 darfst aufstehen – will … vielleicht anschauen / untersuchen
4 Darf ich … gehen? – darfst nicht
5 Darf Ann vorbeikommen …? – Vielleicht wirst du …

Das Datum von heute ____________

166 Modale Hilfsverben – be able, be allowed to

Lies dir zunächst die Dialoge und Sätze sorgfältig durch und kreuze dann die richtige Lösung an. Es gibt jeweils nur eine mögliche Antwort.

can / could, be able to, be allowed to

1 – Julia is allowed to speak ○ can speak ○ German.
– You're right. She'll be allowed to help ○ 'll be able to help ○ us when the German visitors are here.

2 My father says I couldn't go ○ can't go ○ on the trip unless I do better at school. If I don't, he won't give his permission and I won't be allowed to come ○ am not able to come ○.

3 I was lucky yesterday. Mum phoned the hospital and they said I could come ○ can come ○ at once. They can see ○ were able to see ○ me because another patient couldn't come ○ can't come ○.

may / might, be allowed to

4 – Mum, was I allowed to get up ○ may I get up ○ now?
– Not today, but Dr Pill said you might not watch ○ will be allowed to watch ○ television for a couple of hours tomorrow.

5 – Alison said she may come ○ might come ○ out this evening, but she has got so much to do that she may not have ○ isn't allowed to have ○ the time. And her dad said she will not be allowed to go ○ may not go ○ out in the evenings for a week.
– Yes, but she wasn't allowed to go ○ may not go ○ out in the evenings last week. She might leave ○ may leave ○ the house now.

1 can speak – 'll be able to help
2 can't go – won't be allowed to come
3 could come – were able to see – couldn't come
4 may I get up – will be allowed to watch
5 might come – may not have – will not be allowed to go – wasn't allowed to go – may/might leave

Das Datum von heute ____________

167 Verschiedene modale Hilfsverben

Übersetze die unterstrichenen Satzteile mithilfe eines geeigneten Hilfsverbs ins Englische. Vergiss nicht, dass du manchmal ein Ersatzhilfsverb benutzen musst.

1 Joe könnte heute Abend kommen, aber ich glaube es nicht.

____

2 Darf ich die Rechnung *(bill)* bitte haben?

____

3 Wenn es warm genug ist, dürfen wir bestimmt schwimmen gehen.

____

4 Wenn du hart arbeitest, wirst du in einem Jahr viel Englisch verstehen können.

____

5 Ich wollte spielen, aber der Arzt sagte, dass ich noch nicht spielen darf.

____

6 Darf ich etwas zu essen haben?

____

Gestern konnte ich nichts essen, aber jetzt fühle ich mich besser.

____

G 7/8

1 might come
2 May I have …?
3 we may go swimming
4 you will be able to understand
5 I am not allowed to play (yet)
6 May I have something to eat? I wasn't able to eat.

Das Datum von heute __________

168 Relativsätze mit Relativpronomen I

Setze *who/that, which/that* oder *whose* ein.

1 Mrs Green is the woman ___who/that___ won the pools *(Lotto)*.

2 Nessie is a monster ___who/that___ lives in Loch Ness.

3 The nice man ___who/that___ works at the café is our uncle.

4 The car ___whose___ radio was stolen belongs to my uncle.

5 That is the man ___which/that___ wife was Miss Wales last year.

6 The bell ___which/that___ is heard on the BBC is Big Ben.

7 We need a dog ___which/that___ will guard the house.

8 The film ___which/that___ won the Oscar was filmed in Ireland.

9 The bagpipes is a musical instrument ___which/that___ is played in the Highlands of Scotland.

2 who/that
3 who/that
4 whose
5 whose
6 which/that
7 which/that
8 which/that
9 which/that

Das Datum von heute ___________

169 Relativsätze mit Relativpronomen II

Pete Brayne zeigt seinen Kindern alte Fotos. Er gibt zu jedem Foto eine Erklärung. Verbinde die Sätze mithilfe eines Relativpronomens.

1 This is a little town in Cornwall. Its name is Portewe.

This is a little town in Cornwall whose name is Portewe.

2 This is Uncle Benjamin. His family has lived in Norfolk for over 300 years.

This is Uncle Benjamin whose family lived in Norfolk for over 300 years.

3 These are some friends. Their home is in Ulster.

These are some friends whose home is in Ulster.

4 This is a part of Scotland. It has beautiful mountains and lakes.

This is a part of Scotland which has beautiful mountains and lakes.

5 This is York. The city gets a lot of visitors every year.

This is York which gets a lot of visitors every year.

6 This is Gareth Evans. His home is in Wales.

This is Gareth Evans whose home is in Wales.

7 This is my school. Its buildings are very old.

This is my school whose buildings are very old.

8 And this is my first girl-friend. Her name was Liz.

This is my first girl-friend whose name was Liz.

2 whose family has lived
3 whose home is
4 which/that has
5 which gets
6 whose home is
7 whose buildings are
8 whose name was

170 Haupt- und Relativsatz

Der Programmierer hat irgendetwas falsch gemacht. Er hat den Hauptsatz und den Relativsatz der Sätze durcheinandergebracht. Benutze die Buchstaben, um die Satzteile richtig zusammenzustellen.

1 Lord Nelson was a great admiral/which is visited by millions of tourists every year. **(A)**
2 London is a city/which is spoken in most parts of Wales. **(B)**
3 Ulster is a part of Britain/who came from Norfolk on the east coast of England. **(C)**
4 Welsh is a difficult language/which is full of beautiful lakes and forests. **(D)**
5 Kent is a farming area of South-East England/who came from Liverpool. **(E)**
6 The Beatles were a famous popgroup/which has big problems at the moment. **(F)**
7 Scotland is the part of Britain/which is sometimes called the 'Garden of England'. **(G)**
8 The Lake District is a region of North-West England/which is famous for Scotch whisky. **(H)**

(1) C (2) __ (3) __ (4) __ (5) __ (6) __ (7) __ (8) __

2 A
3 F
4 B
5 G
6 E
7 H
8 D

Das Datum von heute ___________

171 Relativsätze ohne Relativpronomen (contact clause)

Entscheide dich, ob das Relativpronomen notwendig ist oder nicht. Wenn nicht, bilde einen *contact clause,* indem du das unnötige Relativpronomen durchstreichst.

1 Jim is happy with the new jeans ~~which~~ he bought yesterday.

2 Most of the children ~~that~~ she teaches enjoy her lessons.

3 The lady who won the money went on a world tour.

4 The dog who bit the postman belongs to our neighbour.

5 The steak ~~that~~ I had was awful.

6 Everything ~~that~~ people enjoy most seems to be bad for them.

7 The player who wins the match gets £ 1,000 and a cup *(Pokal).*

8 Mrs Todd always gives us cake ~~which~~ she has made herself.

9 The postcard ~~that~~ we sent from Jersey still hasn't arrived.

2 ~~that~~
3 who
4 who
5 ~~that~~
6 ~~that~~
7 who
8 ~~which~~
9 ~~that~~

G
7/8

Das Datum von heute ___________

172 Relativpronomen oder nicht?

Wo notwendig, setze ein Relativpronomen ein. Sonst lass die Sätze als *contact clauses* stehen.

1 Hollywood is a place ___that___ interests many people.

2 People ___who___ live in Hollywood are not all film stars.

3 Many films ___which___ were made here have become big hits.

4 A film ___________ many people enjoyed was 'E.T.'

5 An actor ___who___ is now very popular is Clint Eastwood.

6 I saw the actress ___who___ made this film yesterday.

7 What is the City ___which___ the Beatles came from?

8 'Mull of Kintyre' is a song ___________ McCartney sings.

9 A TV series ___which___ is very popular is 'Dallas'.

2 who
3 that/which
4 –
5 who
6 who
7 –
8 –
9 which/that

G
7/8

Das Datum von heute __________

173 Reflexivpronomen

Setze die richtigen Reflexivpronomen ein.

1 Jim hasn't got a teacher. He is teaching himself German.

2 Mrs Drew enjoys ______________ at the bingo every week.

3 The cake is on the table. Just help ______________ boys.

4 Pat and Ann are old enough to look after ______________ when we are out.

5 I cut ______________ while I was getting the vegetables ready.

6 'DIY' stands for 'Do it ______________ .

7 Look at that poor bird. I think it's hurt ______________ .

8 You sit down, Mrs Cary. We can get the tea ______________ .

9 Bob didn't buy that cake. He made it ______________ .

10 Alison, Jane, stop being so silly. Behave ______________ .

2 herself
3 yourselves
4 themselves
5 myself
6 yourself
7 itself
8 ourselves
9 himself
10 yourselves

Das Datum von heute __________

174 Verben ohne Reflexivpronomen

Lies die Sätze durch und setze dann die englische Übersetzung der angegebenen deutschen Verben ein. Achte auch auf die Zeiten!

1 The door ___opened___ and a girl came out. (öffnete sich)

2 I ________________ where my glasses are. (wundere mich)

3 Do you ________________ ? We met him last year. (dich erinnern)

4 They ________________________________ before they go to the concert. (werden sich umziehen)

5 I ________________ very well, Mum. (fühle mich nicht)

6 Al always ________________ in the evenings. (rasiert sich)

7 Look at that parked car. It ________________________________. (bewegt sich)

8 What's wrong with Alison? She ________________________ so much during the last few weeks. (hat sich … geändert)

9 The doors only ________________ from the inside. (öffnen sich)

10 The thief ________________ in the woods. (versteckte sich)

2 wonder
3 remember
4 will change/get changed
5 don't feel
6 shaves
7 's moving/moves
8 has changed
9 open
10 hid

G 7/8

175 Each other/one another oder ein Reflexivpronomen

Setze *each other/one another* oder ein Reflexivpronomen ein.

1 The boy fell off his bike and cut ________________ badly.

2 In small villages everyone knows ______________________________________.

3 Penfriends write letters to _________________________________ often to give ________________ practice in a foreign language.

4 Go and look at ____________________ in the mirror. You've got egg on your face.

5 You shouldn't play with ______________________________________ in church.

6 Ben, I'll do that. I'd like to do it ______________________________________.

7 Twins often look like ____ don't they?

8 Mrs Drew and her mother write to ____________________________ every week.

9 If you live alone, you start talking to ________________________ when there is nobody there.

10 In self-service restaurants the customers fetch what they want to eat ______________________________. There are no waiters.

1 himself
2 each other/one another
3 each other/one another – themselves
4 yourself
5 each other/one another
6 myself
7 each other/one another
8 each other/one another
9 yourself
10 themselves

Das Datum von heute ___________

176 Das Stützwort one

Übersetze die unterstrichenen Satzteile ins Englische.

1 – Welche Äpfel willst du?

– Ich will die roten.

the red ones

2 Die blauen Socken sind kürzer als die gelben.

____

3 Diese Häuser sind teurer als die dort drüben.

____

4 Hast du einen neuen Comic? Ich habe alle die alten gelesen.

____

5 Diese Schuhe sind zu klein. Können Sie mir größere zeigen?

____

6 Welche Hosen nimmst du mit? Die blauen oder die braunen?

____

7 Hast du ein Buch mit? Ich habe keins.

____

8 Der Film war viel besser als der letzte Woche.

____

9 Ich finde diese Bluse zu teuer. Haben Sie eine billigere?

____

10 Welches Fahrrad hast du gemeint? Das silberne oder das gelbe?

____

2 than the yellow ones
3 than the ones over there
4 the old ones
5 bigger ones
6 The blue ones or the brown ones?
7 I haven't got one.
8 than the one
9 a cheaper one
10 The silver one or the yellow one?

Das Datum von heute ___________

177 Die Wortstellung: Sätze mit zwei Objekten I

Benutze Ziffern, um die Satzteile in die richtige Reihenfolge zu stellen.

1 (4) a letter (3) her penfriend in Japan (1) Kara (2) wrote

2 ( ) a photo of Witten? ( ) has ( ) her ( ) sent ( ) she

3 ( ) asked ( ) for some information about Japan ( ) her ( ) she

4 ( ) her ( ) taught ( ) three Japanese words ( ) Yuki Ito

5 ( ) so she ( ) three German words ( ) wrote ( ) Yuki Ito

6 ( ) a paper flower ( ) her ( ) made ( ) Yuki Ito

7 ( ) for Christmas ( ) Kara ( ) sent ( ) she ( ) the flower

8 ( ) did ( ) her ( ) is ( ) Kara ( ) reading? ( ) tell ( ) that ( ) her hobby

G 7/8

2 5 1 4 3 2
3 2 4 3 1
4 3 2 4 1
5 1 4 2 3
6 4 3 2 1
7 5 3 2 1 4
8 1 4 7 2 8 3 5 6

Das Datum von heute ____________

178 Die Wortstellung: Sätze mit zwei Objekten II

Bringe die Satzelemente in die richtige Reihenfolge und bilde vollständige Sätze. Achte auf die Wortstellung und die Zeiten!

1 teach/English/German technicians/Paul

Does Paul teach German technicians English on Mondays?

2 his mother/Joe/promise ______________________________ that he would be careful.

3 give/her little cat/Mrs Cary/some fresh fish

____

______________________________________ yesterday.

4 a card/send/their friends/the Todds

____

______________________________________ last Christmas?

5 lies/must not tell/people/you

____

______________________________________ , Joe.

6 her brother/Julie/make/some football socks

____

______________________________________ last week.

7 a letter/we/write you

____

______________________________________ soon.

8 bikes/buy/Mr Pryce/the twins ______________________

______________________________________ last year.

2 Joe promised his mother
3 Mrs Cary gave her little cat some fresh fish
4 Did the Todds send their friends a card …?
5 You must not tell people lies
6 Julie made her brother some football socks
7 We will write you a letter
8 Mr Pryce bought the twins bikes

G 7/8

Das Datum von heute ___________

179 Die Wortstellung: mehrfache Orts- und Zeitadverbien I

In den folgenden Sätzen sind einige Zeit- und Ortsangaben falsch eingesetzt. Benutze Pfeile, um die falschen Sätze zu korrigieren. Alle Satzteile sind unbetont.

1 We had to speak English last summer in Denmark .

2 Luckily my brother can speak English. He is starting a new job in August in India.

3 Tom Jones sang his new hit last night on TV.

4 We are going to spend Christmas in Bristol this year at my parents' house.

5 There was an interview with the Chinese Prime Minister yesterday on the radio.

6 Ann's new flat is at the end of the road in the new house.

7 Let's meet at the pub tonight at about half past seven, OK?

8 Stefan will have to use in the Export Department *(Abteilung)* English next year.

2 in India in August
3 on TV last night
4 at my parents' house in Bristol this year
5 on the radio yesterday
6 in the new house at the end of the road
7 at about half past seven tonight
8 English in the Export Department next year

Das Datum von heute ____________

180 Die Wortstellung: mehrfache Orts- und Zeitadverbien II

Übersetze ins Englische.

1 Gestern sah ich Tom Jones im Fernsehen.

2 Die nächsten Olympischen Spiele sind 2008 in Peking.

3 Mein Vater lernt zu Hause am Wochenende Englisch.

4 Letzte Woche musste ich nach Frankfurt.

5 Gestern sprachen wir beim Abendessen Englisch.

6 Während der Karnevalszeit *(carnival)* fahren wir zu Freunden in Norddeutschland.

1 I saw Tom Jones on TV yesterday.
2 The next Olympic Games will be in Peking in 2008.
3 My father learns English at home at the weekends.
4 I had to go to Frankfurt last week.
5 We spoke English at supper yesterday.
6 We go to friends in North Germany during carnival.

G 7/8

Das Datum von heute ___________

181 Die Wortstellung: Adverbien der Häufigkeit und des Grades I

Benutze einen Pfeil, um das angegebene Adverb an die richtige Stelle zu setzen.

1 My brother works at the weekend. (sometimes)

2 Mr Todd gets home before 10 o'clock. (always)

3 The lesson has begun. (just)

4 Alison goes out with Brian. (still) (now and then)

5 Most American workers get two weeks holiday. (only)

6 Julie should be careful. She knows the man. (hardly)

7 Ben is late for evening class. (often)

8 We go to the cinema. (once a week)

1 My brother sometimes works …
2 Mr Todd always gets home …
3 The lesson has just begun.
4 Alison still goes out with Brain now and then.
5 Most American workers only get …
6 She hardly knows …
7 Ben is often late …
8 We go to the cinema once a week.

G 7/8

182 Die Wortstellung: Adverbien der Häufigkeit und des Grades II

Übersetze ins Englische.

1 Bernd kann kaum laufen.

Bernd ____

2 Einmal im Monat besuchen wir meinen Opa.

We ____

3 In England gibt es nur acht Feiertage *(public holidays)* im Jahr.

In England there ____

4 Ab und zu sehe ich Max im Büro *(at the office)*.

I ____

5 Manchmal finde ich Fußball ganz unterhaltsam.

I ____

6 – Beeil dich! Du bist immer so langsam!

Hurry up! You ____

– O.k. Ich bin fast fertig.

O.k. ____

1 (Bernd) can hardly walk.
2 (We) visit my grandad once a month.
3 (In England there) are only eight public holidays a/each year.
4 (I) see Max at the office now and then.
5 (I) sometimes find football quite entertaining.
6 – (Hurry up!) You are always so slow.
– (OK.) I am ('m) nearly ready.

183 Verschiedene Satzelemente

Bilde vollständige Sätze mit den angegebenen Satzelementen. Achte auf die Wortstellung und die Zeiten! In einigen Fällen musst du außerdem Artikel und/oder Präposition ergänzen.

1 Mike/go/Australia/usually/winter

Mike usually goes to Australia in winter.

2 Pat and Jenny/meet/always/park/Sunday afternoons

Pat and Jenny ______________________________

______________________________.

3 I / listen/world news/hour ago/radio

I ______________________________

______________________________.

4 We can see/films in English/often/TV

We ______________________________

______________________________.

5 Some New Yorkers/go out/alone at night/seldom

Some New Yorkers ______________________________

______________________________.

6 You/must be/quiet/between 1 and 3/always/Germany/afternoon

You ______________________________

______________________________.

7 Some parts/Holland/people/can watch/TV/four different countries/evening/sometimes

In some parts of Holland people ______________________________

____

______________________________.

2 (Pat and Jenny) always meet in the park on Sunday afternoons.
3 (I) listened to the world news on the radio an hour ago.
4 (We) can often see films in English on TV.
5 (Some New Yorkers) seldom go out alone at night.
6 (You) must always be quiet in Germany between 1 and 3 in the afternoon.
7 … can sometimes watch TV from four different countries in the evening.

184 Mengenangaben

Joe, Ben, Pat und Ann wollen eine Party geben. Zunächst stellen sie fest, was sie schon haben und was sie noch besorgen müssen. Vervollständige den Dialog mit den Mengenangaben unten. Es gibt nur eine richtige Lösung:

a lot of *(3 x)* – any – how many *(2 x)* – how much – many – much *(2 x)* – not much – plenty – plenty of – some *(4 x)*

Ann We've got quite ________________ [1] lemonade.

Pat Yes, but ________________ [2] coke have we got?

Ann ________________ [3]. We've only got two bottles.

Joe OK, I'll get ________________ [4] coke on my way home from school. ________________ [5] bottles do we need?

Pat Twelve.

Ben Twelve? Good heavens, ________________ [6] people are coming to the party? That's too ________________ [7]. We've got ________________ [8] lemonade already. We don't need so ________________ [9] coke. Six bottles will be ________________ [10].

Joe Ben's right. We haven't got ________________ [11] money, either, and we still need ________________ [12] food, don't we?

Ann Yes, of course. We've got ________________ [13] nuts left from Christmas, but it would be nice to have ________________ [14] cheese and ham as well.

Pat I'll ask my mum. I don't think we've got ________________ [15] ham at home, but we've got ________________ [16] cheese, so I'm sure she'll give us ________________ [17].

1 a lot of
2 how much
3 Not much
4 some
5 How many
6 how many
7 many
8 a lot of
9 much
10 plenty
11 much
12 some
13 plenty of
14 some
15 any
16 a lot of
17 some

185 A little/a few

Vervollständige das Kochrezept mit *a little/a few*

An easy omelette

Ingredients *(Zutaten)*

____________ [1] eggs (three for an ordinary omelette, four if you are ____________ [2] hungrier), ____________ [3] spoonfuls of fresh milk, ____________ [4] butter, ____________ [5] salt and pepper (if you like).

What to do

- Put the butter into a clean frying-pan, and heat for ____________ [6] minutes. Break the eggs into a bowl and beat them ____________ [7] times with a whisk. Add the milk and beat the mixture ____________ [8] more. Add ____________ [9] pinches *(Prise)* of salt and ____________ [10] white pepper, if liked. Stir again.
- Pour the mixture into the heated pan (not too hot!) and let it cook for one or two minutes. Turn the omelette over, and cook on other side for ____________ [11] seconds. (If you like, you can put ____________ [12] cheese or ____________ [13] small bits of ham into the omelette before you turn it over.)
- Take the omelette carefully out of the pan and leave to cool for ____________ [14] time before you eat it.

1 a few
2 a little
3 a few
4 a little
5 a little
6 a few
7 a few
8 a little
9 a few
10 a little
11 a few
12 a little
13 a few
14 a little

186 Das Passiv im simple present

Vervollständige den folgenden Bericht, indem du *is/are* + Partizip (3. Form) einsetzt.

Do you know how a hit record __is made__ [1] (make)? Well, first the song ____________ [2] (write) and a good group ____________ [3] (found). Sometimes the singers ____________ [4] (know), but quite often they ____________ [5] (not know). Then the song ____________ [6] (record) without the band. The words alone ____________ [7] (put) onto a tape. If the group isn't very good, the tape ____________ [8] (improve) by Studio technicians. Later a professional band ____________ [9] (ask) to fill in the music. The music ____________ [10] (sometimes/play) by very good musicians from symphony orchestras. Then all the radio stations ____________ [11] (give) a copy of the new record. They ____________ [12] (often/pay) a lot of money to play it ____________ [13] (sell) in all the record shops.

2 is written
3 is found
4 are known
5 are not known
6 is recorded
7 are put
8 is improved
9 is asked
10 is sometimes played
11 are given
12 are often paid
13 is sold

Das Datum von heute __________

187 Das Passiv im simple past

Setze die angegebenen Verben ein. Benutze dabei die Passivform des *simple past*.

Yesterday there was nearly a tragedy in Duke Street. Five-year-old Mandy Cooper was hit [1] (hit) by a car and ____________________ [2] (throw) into the path of a bus coming in the other direction. Luckily, Mandy ____________________ [3] (not run) over. She was small enough to go between the wheels of the bus. The car driver did not stop, but the car ____________________ [4] (soon/find) by the police. It ____________________ [5] (hid) in a garage in Rose Lane. The owner of the car ____________________ [6] (take) to the police station, but he ____________________ [7] (allow) to go home again. His car ____________________ [8] (steal) by someone early yesterday morning. Mandy ____________________ [9] (drive) to hospital in a police car. Doctors said last night that she was 'as well as ____________________ [10] (can expect)'. They added, however, that she ____________________ ____________________ [11] (very badly/not injure).

2 (was) thrown
3 was not run
4 was soon found
5 was hidden
6 was taken
7 was allowed
8 was / had been stolen
9 was driven
10 could be expected
11 was not very badly injured

Das Datum von heute ____________

188 Passivformen in verschiedenen Zeiten

Setze die angegebenen Verben ein. Benutze durchweg das Passiv.
Beachte, dass alle Zeiten in dieser Übung vorkommen.

1 – Little Johnny Brown ____________________ (not see) since last Tuesday. Do you think he ____________________ (kidnap)?
– Don't be silly. He ____________________ (collect) by his uncle and aunt. He has gone on holiday with them.

2 The supermarket ____________________ (break) into last night, and over £ 5,000 ____________________ (steal). Hundreds of cars ____________________ (stop), but the thief still ____________________ (not find).

3 Next week the winner of the competition ____________________ (drive) to London in a Rolls-Royce and he – or she – ____________________ (welcome) to the best hotel in town by a famous TV star.

4 Soft drinks ____________________ (can buy) at that kiosk over there.

5 Radios ____________________ (should not play) on the beach.

6 – French and German ____________________ (teach) at British schools, but French ____________________ (learn) by more pupils than German.
– Yes, that's why only a few partners ____________________ (can find) by German pupils.

1 hasn't been seen – has been kidnapped – was / has been collected
2 was broken – were stolen – were stopped – hasn't been found
3 will be driven – will be welcomed
4 can be bought
5 should not be played
6 are taught – is learnt / learned – can be found

G 7/8

Das Datum von heute ____________

189 Vom Aktivsatz zum Passivsatz

Stelle diese Aktivsätze ins Passiv um.

1 Somebody stole Julie's purse at school today.

Julie's purse was stolen at school today.

2 One day doctors will find a cure for cancer.

One day ____

3 Somebody has painted horrible pictures on the walls.

____

on the walls.

4 A man paid a million pounds for a Picasso last week.

____

for a Picasso last week.

5 They are going to build a motorway through the village.

____

through the village.

6 A businessman has already sold London Bridge to an American.

____

to an American.

7 Someone is going to teach Italian at our school.

____

at our school.

2 … a cure for cancer will be found.
3 Horrible pictures have been painted …
4 A million pounds was paid …
5 A motorway is going to be built …
6 London Bridge has already been sold
7 Italian is going to be taught …

190 If-Sätze: Aussagesätze I

Es gibt drei Arten von *if*-Sätzen, die alle verschiedene Zeiten aufweisen:

Typ	*if*-Teil	Hauptteil
1	simple present	will-future
2	simple past	would + infinitive *(Grundform)*
3	past perfect	would have + participle *(3. Form)*

Schreibe in die Kästchen am Ende des Satzes, um welche Art *if*-Satz es sich handelt.

1 If you are not there, we'll wait outside the cafe. (1)

2 We would go on holiday if we had enough money. ( )

3 We'll see you at Ann's party if we go. ( )

4 If you had practised more, you would have done better. ( )

5 If Mr Bunn was friendly, he would get more customers. ( )

6 The Indians wouldn't have attacked the settlers if the settlers hadn't stolen their land. ( )

7 Columbus said, 'If we sail to the West, we will find land.' ( )

8 If I'm there first, I'll get a table near the band. ( )

2 2
3 1
4 3
5 2
6 3
7 1
8 1

Das Datum von heute __________

191 *If*-Sätze: Aussagesätze II

Vervollständige die *if*-Sätze.

Typ 1

1 If the weather _is_ good, we _will go camping_ at the weekend. (be/go camping)

2 If I __________ a holiday job, I __________ some money. (get/earn)

3 The Indians said, 'We __________ nothing to eat if you __________ all the buffaloes.' (have/kill)

Typ 2

4 If the taxi-driver __________ faster, we __________ at the station on time. (drive/arrive)

5 A lot of pupils __________ better at school if they __________ to the teacher. (do/listen)

6 If the settlers __________ to understand the Indians, they __________ together peacefully. (try/live)

Typ 3

7 I'm sure that Mr Bunn __________ Brian a job if he __________ more polite to him. (give/be)

8 If the white settlers __________ their promises, the Indians __________ them alone. (keep/leave)

9 We __________ the match if we __________ harder. (win/practise)

2 get – will earn
3 will have – kill
4 drove – would arrive
5 would do – listened
6 tried – would live
7 would have given – had been
8 had kept – would have left
9 would have won – had practised

G 7/8

192 If-Sätze: Verneinte Sätze und Fragen

Verbinde die links aufgelisteten Satzteile mit den Teilen rechts, um sinnvolle *if*-Sätze zu bilden.

1 If you had done your homework,	____	thousands of Indians would not have died of hunger.
2 If you don't prepare for the test properly,	____	the tribes would live at peace with the settlers.
3 Would you lend me your new CD	____	if you had had some food at home?
4 If the settlers didn't destroy the forests,	____	we won't go on holiday this year.
5 Will you help me later	____	if I gave you these comics?
6 If the farmers hadn't killed the buffalo,	1	the teacher wouldn't have been so angry.
7 Would you have eaten at an expensive restaurant	____	if I help you now?
8 If my dad doesn't find a job,	____	of course you won't do well.

2 of course you won't do well.
3 if I gave you these comics?
4 the tribes would live at peace with the settlers.
5 if I help you now?
6 thousands of Indians would not have died of hunger
7 if you had had some food at home?
8 we won't go on holiday this year.

Das Datum von heute ____________

193 Drei Arten von if-Sätzen

Lies die Dialoge sorgfältig durch und entscheide, um welchen Satztyp es sich handelt. Dann setze die Verben ein.

1 – It was lucky that the ambulance came so quickly yesterday.

– Yes. If it had not come (not come) at once, old Mrs Cary ______________________ (die).

2 – Syd is horrible. He's so rude and bad-tempered. But he'll never change *(sich verändern).*

– Yes, but if he __________ (be) nicer, he ______________________ (have) a much easier life.

3 – Come on, Jack. If we ______________________ (not leave) now, we ______________________ (be) late again.

– OK. Let's go.

4 – Mrs Green's parrot bit me today.

– Yes, but it was your fault. If you ______________________ (not put) your finger into his cage, he ______________________ (not bite) you.

5 – If the settlers ______________________ (find) oil on the Sioux's land, the army ______________________ (put) them in a reservation, too.

– I know. That's what happened to a lot of tribes.

6 – Millions of Irish people went to live in the USA during the 19th century.

– Yes. If life in Ireland ______________________ (not be) so hard, they ______________________ (stay) at home.

– Oh, I don't know. If I ______________________ (have) the chance, I ______________________ (like) to live in the USA.

– Yes, but that won't happen, will it?

G 7/8

1 (had not come) – would have died
2 was – would have
3 don't leave – will be
4 hadn't put – would not have bitten
5 had found – would have put
6 hadn't been – would have stayed – had – would like

194 Indirekte Rede I

Setze die folgenden direkten Äußerungen in die indirekte Rede. Benutze dabei jeweils das angegebene *introductory verb*.

1 *Mr Todd* 'I enjoyed the picnic very much.' (say)

Mr Todd said (that) he had enjoyed the picnic very much.

2 *Alison* 'Joe is an awful boy. He put a frog in my bed.' (shout)

Alison shouted (that) Joe saw an awful boy because he had put a frog in her bed.

3 *Mr Todd* 'Alison is just too serious. Of course Joe likes playing tricks on her.' (think)

Mr Todd thought (that) Alison was too serious, so of course Joe liked playing tricks on her.

4 *Mrs Todd* 'Joe, I am pleased you help old Mrs Cary with her shopping so often.' (tell)

Mrs Todd told Joe (that) she was pleased (that) he helped old Mrs Cary with her shopping so often.

5 *Joe* 'I'll wait for you outside the café Ben.' (promise)

Joe promised (that) he would wait for Ben outside the café.

6 *MrsTodd* 'Joe, Alison will be very angry with you if you play with her make-up again.' (say)

Mrs Todd said (that) Alison would be very angry with Joe if he played with her make-up again.

2 shouted – was – had put
3 thought – was – liked
4 told Joe – was – helped
5 promised – would wait
6 said – would be – played

Das Datum von heute ____________

195 Indirekte Rede II

Lies den Dialog durch und setze dann die fehlenden Wörter und Ausdrücke in den Bericht ein. Beachte dabei die Änderungen, die bei der indirekten Rede notwendig sind.

Mrs Todd Joe dear, I want you to come straight home from school today. We're visiting Aunt Mabel in hospital.
Joe But I'm going to the cinema with Ben this afternoon. I can't come.
Alison You're coming, Joe. You'll just have to go to the cinema or something.
Joe That'll be too late. The film changes tomorrow.
Mr Todd Look, Joe, you were happy enough to see Aunt Mabel last Christmas when she gave you those lovely presents, weren't you? You had plenty of time then, didn't you?
Well, now you can at least visit her when she is ill in hospital, OK?

Mrs Todd __told__ [1] Joe that __she__ [2] wanted __him__ [3] to come straight home from school because __they wanted__ [4] to visit his Aunt Mabel in hospital. But Joe answered that he __could not come__ [5]. He __said__ [6] that __he__ [7] was going to the cinema with his friend Ben __that afternoon__ [8]. Alison __told__ [9] Joe that __he__ [10] was __coming__ [11] to the hospital. She __said__ [12] that he __would__ [13] just __have to go__ [14] to the cinema __the next day__ [15].
Joe replied that that __it would be__ [16] too late as the film __changed__ [17] the __changing days__ [18]. Then his father __said__ [19] that Joe __had been__ [20] happy enough to see Aunt Mabel ____________ [21] when she __had given__ [22] him a lot of presents. Mr Todd said that Joe __had had__ [23] plenty of time then. Finally, Joe's father told him that he __could__ [24] at least visit __his aunt__ [25] when she __was__ [26] ill in hospital.

2 she
3 him
4 they wanted
5 could not come
6 said
7 he
8 that afternoon
9 told
10 he
11 coming
12 suggested
13 would
14 have to go
15 the next day
16 would be
17 changed
18 following day
19 said
20 had been
21 the previous Christmas
22 had given
23 had had
24 could
25 his aunt / her
26 was

G 7/8

Das Datum von heute ___________

196 Indirekte Fragen

Schreibe die Fragen unten in indirekte Fragen um. Benutze durchweg *if* bzw. *whether*, und denke an alle Änderungen, die du durchführen musst.

1 *Pat* 'Are they going to the dance tonight?'

Pat asked if (whether) they were going to the dance that night.

2 *Ann* 'Has she seen the new film at the ABC yet?'

Ann ______________________________

the new film at the ABC ______________________________.

3 *Jim* 'Did you hear the weather forecast yesterday, Eve?'

Jim ______________ Eve ______________________________

______________________________.

4 *Tim* 'Do they like steaks?'

Tim ______________________________ steaks.

5 *Eve* 'Pat, can you get me some tea tomorrow?'

Eve ______________ Pat ______________________________

some tea ______________________________.

6 *Ben* 'Do we have to go to school next week?'

Ben ______________________________

to school ______________________________.

2 asked if / whether she had seen … yet.
3 asked … if / whether she had heard the weather forecast the previous day.
4 asked if / whether they liked …
5 aked … if / whether she could get her … the next day.
6 asked if / whether they had to go … the following week.

G 7/8

Das Datum von heute ________

197 Indirekte Befehle und Bitten

Gib die Anweisungen der Polizeibeamten in der indirekten Rede wieder. Mit wem gesprochen wird, steht jeweils in Klammern am Satzende. Wenn *please* im Satz steht, benutze *asked*, sonst *told*.

1 *PC Davis* 'Move along, please.' (pedestrians)

PC Davis asked the pedestrians to move along.

2 *PC Smith* 'Don't touch anything.' (small boy)

PC Smith ________________________________

________________________________.

3 *PC Green* 'Let the ambulance through.' (some women)

PC Green ________________________________

________________________________.

4 *PC Smith* 'Go home.' (everyone)

PC Smith ________________________________

5 *PC Green* 'Give me your name and address, please.' (Mrs Cary)

PC Green ________________________________

________________________________.

6 *PC Davis* 'Clean the blood off the road, please.' (a worker)

PC Davis ________________________________.

7 *PC Smith* 'Don't smoke.' (a man)

PC Smith ________________________________

PC = Police Constable

G 7/8

2 told the small boy not to touch anything.
3 told some women to let the ambulance through.
4 told everyone to go home.
5 asked Mrs Cary to give him her name and address.
6 asked a worker to clean the blood off the road.
7 told a man not to smoke.

Das Datum von heute ____________

198 Präpositionen

Manfred aus Nordhessen, Birgit aus Salzburg und Lars aus Hamburg haben alle Brieffreunde in England gefunden. Sie schreiben ihren Brieffreunden etwas über die Gegend, in der sie wohnen. Lies dir die Briefauszüge durch und setze die fehlenden Präpositionen ein.

1 My name is Manfred, and I live ________ Vöhl, a small village ________ the Edersee ________ the eastern part ________ Hesse ________ West Germany. Vöhl is ________ the small towns Frankenberg and Korbach. You can drive ________ Kassel, which is the biggest town ________ our region in about an hour.

2 My name is Birgit. I come ________ Salzburg ________ the Austrian Tyrol. Mozart came ________ the city; and you can still go ________ the house where he was born. There are beautiful mountains and forests all ________ Salzburg, and tourists come here ________ all over the world to walk t________ the forests and to climb u________ the mountains.

3 My name is Lars Petersen, and I live ________ Hamburg, a big port ________ the Elbe ________ North Germany. We live ________ a part ________ Hamburg called Winterhude. The river Alster is ________ the end ________ our road. You can go ________ boat d________ the river and a____________________ a big lake which is also called the Alster. You can get out ________ the boat right ________ the middle ________ the city.

1 in – near – in – of – in – near – of – to – in
2 from – in – from – to – around – from – through – up
3 in – on – in – in – of – at – of – by – down – along / across – of – in – of

G 7/8

Das Datum von heute ____________

199 Feste Adjektiv-Präposition-Verbindungen

Setze die Präpositionen ein.

– I'm really bored ________ [1] Martin.

– Oh? Why?

– Well, I said I'm good ________ [2] sport, so he immediately said that he's good ________ [3] sport, too.

– So what? What are you so annoyed ________ [4]? Martin's not bad ________ [5] sport, is he?

– Yes, but that's not what I mean. Look, I said I'm worried ________ [6] the German test, right? Then he says he's nervous ________ [7] it, too. I'm interested ________ [8] flying, and Martin? He's excited ________ [9] planes as well. I say I'm glad ________ [10] this and that. And what does Martin say? Go on, guess.

– Well, I suppose he says he's happy ________ [11] this and that, too.

– You're right. Why can't he be different ________ [12] me?
I get so tired ________ [13] it.

– Well, that's the trouble with twin brothers, isn't it?

1 with
2 at
3 at
4 about
5 at
6 about
7 about
8 in
9 about
10 about
11 about
12 from
13 of

G 7/8